D1391489

THE
DAMBUSTERS

THE
DAMBUSTERS

JOHN SWEETMAN
David Coward and Gary Johnstone

EAST SUSSEX COUNTY LIBRARY	
02768622	
H J	080140
940.5449 ∪	£15.00
6|03	MC

A *Time Warner* Book

First published in Great Britain in 2003 by
Time Warner Books

Copyright © 2003 John Sweetman
Copyright © 2003 David Coward and Gary Johnstone

The moral right of the authors has been asserted.

All rights reserved.
No part of this publication may be reproduced,
stored in a retrieval system, or transmitted, in any
form or by any means, without the prior
permission in writing of the publisher, nor be
otherwise circulated in any form of binding or
cover other than that in which it is published and
without a similar condition including this
condition being imposed on the subsequent purchaser.

A CIP catalogue record for this book
is available from the British Library.

ISBN 0 316 72618 4

Designed by Barnett Design Consultants Ltd

Printed and bound in Great Britain by
Bath Press Colourbooks, Glasgow

Time Warner Books UK
Brettenham House
Lancaster Place
London WC2E 7EN

www.TimeWarnerBooks.co.uk

Contents

Author's Acknowledgements

Even for a well-known operation like the Dambusters Raid, research remains continuous. Broadly, there are five sources of information: official documents (like Air Ministry records); private papers (letters and diaries); personal memories (gleaned through interview and correspondence); photographs (aerial reconnaissance, still and moving images); and publications (newspapers, journals and books). Concentration on purely British material would present a partial picture, so the archives of other countries and the impressions of their citizens need to be trawled as well. Memories fluctuate, though, records are not comprehensive and many have simply not survived.

Every researcher requires help, guidance and, above all, detached criticism. I remain deeply indebted to the many individuals (not least, those who took part in or were closely associated with Operation Chastise) and organisations, too many to list, which have supplied me with a vast amount of data, patiently answered my queries in the past and continue to do so today. However, I must single out the late Dick Collins (former Road Research Laboratory scientist) who gave me immeasurable advice and assistance, when I began examining the operation, Sir Barnes Wallis's family and 617 Squadron Association, especially its official historian Robert Owen, who have been particularly supportive. The staff of the PRO at Kew, RAF Museum Hendon, Imperial War Museum, Ministry of Defence's Air Historical Branch, Bundesarchiv and different German dams' authorities have all provided unstinting professional and prompt assistance. Finally, Tigress Productions has generously made available the transcripts of interviews with H.R. Humphries, F.E. Sutherland, R. E. Grayston and G. L. Johnson, which have enabled me to fill some of the remaining gaps in my knowledge.

What follows is an account of the search for a way to destroy, in Guy Gibson's words, 'the great dams of Germany', based upon these sources.

Producer's Acknowledgements

Neither the television programmes nor the wealth of new material in this book would have been possible without the support of many people. We are especially indebted to the Royal Air Force, particularly to Air Marshal Paul Thomas MBE and Marcia Nash, as well as the Royal Air Force College, Cranwell, 18 Sqn RAF, 45 (R) Sqn RAF, and 617 Sqn RAF.

Huge thanks to Al, Andy, Branty, Frankie, Lucy, Molly, Tapper and Teri for volunteering for this project and for the credit they have reflected on the RAF and the Dambusters. And, of course, the real members of AJ-N who helped us: to Ray Grayston, to E. C. 'Johnny' Johnson, who sadly passed away in autumn 2002, and Fred 'Doc' Sutherland.

Thank you to Air Commodore John Langston CBE and the 617 Squadron Aircrew Association, whose official historian Robert Owen has been a valued consultant, and thanks also to the Secretary, Ted Wass. Many thanks also to Dr John Sweetman, who is hereby acknowledged in his own book!

We are grateful to Kenji Takeda and his team at Southampton University, especially Al Brizell, for building a magnificent simulator, and to Pat Bill for designing a magnificent set. We'd also like to thank Mungo Amyatt-Leir and all his software geniuses at 'Just Flight' for their dedication to giving life to the Dambusters Raids in the form of a computer game, and thanks to Microsoft.

QinetiQ provided valuable help and advice in the structuring of the programmes, as well as allowing us to expose Arthur Kearse to the media. Bob Wodehouse has provided valuable engineering advice on dam structures, as has Kuldeep Virdi at City University.

Many thanks to Peter Elliot, Andrew Cormack and Ian Thirsk at the Royal Air Force Museum, and Gary Oakley at the Australian War Memorial, for their advice and expertise and for trusting us with their precious artefacts. Not for the first or last time we are very grateful to Paul Sargent at the Department of Film at the Imperial War Museum for his support and assistance in making available previously unseen footage of 'Upkeep' Trials and colour footage of Guy Gibson.

Many thanks to former members of 617 Squadron, 5 Group and the RAF, their friends and relatives, for trusting us with their stories and lending us precious film and photographs: Dr Malcolm Arthurton, Ron Batson, Arthur Boothe, Ken Brown, John Bryden, Phillip Canning, George Chalmers, Joan Clark, Nora Cook, Larry Curtis, Derek Dobbs, Air Marshal Sir Eric Dunn, John Elliott, Jerry Fray, Sid Geater, Fay Gillon, Vic Gill, Nora Hall, Daniel Hobday, Tom Hocker, Harry Humphries, Clive Jeffries, G. E. 'Johnny' Johnson, Philip Johnson, John Edward Jones, Patti Roger Kirkpatrick, John Knight, Olwen Lennon, Grant MacDonald, Alex McKie, Les Munro, Vera Newton, Beck Parsons, Ray and Rose Pittams, Dave Rodger, Kenneth Sandwell, Albert Sanson and Jack Sockett.

We are also very grateful to Diana Barnato Walker, Lettice Curtis, Lionel Dimmery, and Anne Welsh of the Air Transport Auxiliary Association.

Peter Clegg and Margaret Dove have been extremely helpful in providing us with invaluable information and contacts. Many thanks to Peter Rix of the Barnes Wallis Memorial Trust for his advice and support.

There are many enthusiasts and researchers for Bomber Command in general and 617 Squadron in particular who have kindly shared their expertise and resources with us: Alex Bateman, Jim Shortland, Steve Silburn, and Lionel at Flame costume hire. Thanks to Jeremy Hall for the loan of part a Lancaster fuselage. Thanks to the Panton family at the East Kirby-based Lincolnshire Aviation Heritage Museum, and to the Petwood Hotel.

Thanks to photographers Ken Woroner, Andrew Hasson and Stuart Woods. Also to Mrs G. M. Cozens and David Finch for their assistance with the beautiful *Nightbombers* film.

In Germany we are very grateful for the support of Herr Fruke and Marco Drebes at the Wasser und Schifffahrtsamt Hannover-Münden, and Christian Heitfuss of the Ruhrverband.

In Canada we very grateful by the assistance of Canadian Warplane, especially Rick Franks, Pam Rickards, Don Schoffield and all the lovely pilots who volunteer there. Thanks to Malcolm Howland for exhilarating us in England. Many thanks to Meridian Studios for their dedication, support and professionalism, managed by ex-Dambuster Ken Dawkins. And finally many thanks to our fantastic crew – Chris King, Freddie Claire, Tom Legge, Rick Aplin, Catti Calthrop, Isobel Johnstone – and the Tigress production team – Ceri Barnes, Lynsey Neale, Martin Thompson, Kate Parker, Elaine Foster, Max Williams and executive producers David McNab and Jeremy Bradshaw.

Author's Preface

Birth of a Legend

'This is London. The Air Ministry have just issued the following communiqué. In the early hours of this morning, a force of Lancasters of Bomber Command led by Wing Commander G. P. Gibson DSO DFC attacked with mines the dams of the Möhne and Sorpe reservoirs. These control two-thirds of the water storage capacity of the Ruhr Basin.' The BBC news broadcast on Monday 17 May 1943 further explained that the Möhne Dam had been breached 'over a length of 100 yards', as had the Eder Dam further east, 'which controls the head waters of the Weser and Fulda valleys'. Several power stations had been destroyed, and 'photographs show the river below the dams in full flood. The attacks were pressed home from a very low level with great determination and coolness in the face of fierce resistance. Eight of the Lancasters are missing.'

These measured words revealed to eager listeners that the Dambusters Raid had taken place. They were the calm prelude to a prolonged and extensive eruption of unrestrained excitement. The next day, and with mounting fervour on succeeding days, national and provincial newspapers, rapidly followed by weekly and monthly magazines, published banner headlines, penned glowing editorials and detailed accounts enlivened by interviews with aircrew who flew on the raid. Celebratory cartoons and explanatory diagrams soon appeared to illustrate the seemingly endless columns of newsprint devoted to the operation. Members of both Houses paid generous tribute in Parliament, Government Ministers enthused in public and in closed sessions of the War Cabinet. Dramatic aerial photographs of the shattered dams and the scenes of destruction as water rushed downstream provided visual proof of success.

The Lancaster crews had indeed left chaos and confusion behind them, assessed by German authorities in the area of both the Möhne and Eder dams at 'millions of

Reichsmarks' of damage. The effect on individuals was marked, too. At Neheim-Hüsten in the Möhne valley, a conscripted Dutch worker (L. J. H. Hoesen) stood on a bridge watching the distant display of military fireworks and the defences 'having a go'. Hearing an 'appalling explosion', he was puzzled by 'a violent rushing sound', which he suddenly realised was the swollen river speeding towards him. Shouting to those on the bridge with him to get away, he ran up the adjoining hill, pausing to look back when safe. 'I saw the water, with tremendous flood, had swept away the bridge with all the people on it. At the same moment there was a tremendous flash: the power station had also been washed away together with houses and streets.' In the valley below the broken Eder Dam, one village resident 'immediately leapt into the cellar and called: "The dam is broken, everybody out of the cellar. The water is coming,"' before grabbing his youngest child and, like Hoesen, escaping to high ground.

Meanwhile, in England, Air Chief Marshal (ACM) Sir Arthur Harris (Commander-in-Chief, RAF Bomber Command) had phoned his superior, the Chief of the Air Staff (CAS), then in Washington, who in turn had informed the Prime Minister, Winston Churchill, also there for an Allied planning conference. Accounts of the operation, the photos and transcripts of interviews were relayed round the world. In the United States the press and radio stations proved wildly enthusiastic, and Churchill was loudly applauded when he mentioned the achievement in a speech to the joint Houses of Congress two days later. From Joseph Stalin in Moscow and President Roosevelt in the White House came official, congratulatory messages. When leaflets were dropped on Europe describing the raid, communication came via resistance networks of the unmitigated joy expressed by the suffering citizens of occupied countries.

Long after these events, the Dambusters Raid still commands wide attention. Crowds flock to commemorative events, documentaries continue to be made about it, and the box-office hit of 1955 frequently appears on TV. In 1997 rumours that the last remaining scale model of the Möhne Dam near Watford, used for early exploratory experiments, was either to be knocked down or moved, and the recovery of different sizes of practice weapons from the Thames estuary, created vast media interest. So did the announcement in 1998 that the large water tanks at the National Physical Laboratory, Teddington, in which other important tests were carried out, would be demolished.

For most people in the twenty-first century, knowledge of what happened during the night of 16-17 May 1943, of the lengthy lead-up to that operation and its short-term and long-term impact, have been heavily influenced by the film starring Richard Todd as Guy Gibson. That film, as its producer admitted to the aeronautical engineer Barnes Wallis, who perfected the weapon of destruction, concentrated on a strong, single story-line and was primarily a commercial venture: 'a somewhat simplified treatment of highly complicated issues ... we have so little time ... [for] an uninstructed audience'. It was not an accurate account of the raid and was further hampered by security restrictions in force during its production. Yet it remains widely regarded as the authentic version of events. The romantic notion that Gibson thought of using spotlights to judge altitude while watching chorus girls high-kicking in a theatre pales beside the reality that a civilian scientist painstakingly devised the method. In practice, the Lancaster crews soon realised that the flimsy triangular hand-held bomb-sight was unsatisfactory, and several worked out alternative means of calculating the distance at which their depth-charge (neither a bomb nor mine) should be dropped. The film, too, failed to cover the Eder or Sorpe dams and did not credit the correct aircraft with breaching the Möhne Dam. It wrongly depicted the spectacular crash of one of the attacking aircraft beyond a hill at the Eder Dam. Two interesting but often misleading books, Brickhill's *The Dam Busters* and Gibson's *Enemy Coast Ahead* (published posthumously), have reinforced the accepted inaccuracies.

Of the 133 aircrew who flew on the night, eighty-nine were British, twenty-eight Canadian, thirteen Australian, two New Zealanders, and one American. Many were trained under the Empire Training Scheme in South Africa and Rhodesia or incognito in the USA before that country entered the war. Gibson was born in India, his station commander in Argentina. The operation, therefore, had a distinctly international flavour. In reality, too, a wide range of civilian and Service personnel had been striving for a way to destroy the dams long before Wallis became actively involved. When he did, they were by no means all obstructive and unhelpful. Apart from flashes of irritation at examples of bureaucratic lethargy (during July 1942 concerning 'the profound effect of water impact on waves … the Air Staff have been singularly stupid'), Wallis generously and personally acknowledged the assistance that he received. In November 1940 he was 'deeply disturbed' to learn that Air Vice-Marshal (AVM) A. W. Tedder was leaving the Ministry of Aircraft Production (MAP), and thanked him warmly for 'the encouragement and support which you have so consistently given me'.

The 617 Squadron crews who carried out Operation Chastise (the codename for the Dambusters Raid) were aged between 20 and 32, from diverse backgrounds and not all highly decorated. Six of the pilots had no awards, and many of the aircrew had not even completed one tour of operations. The story of the Dambusters Raid was indeed 'highly complicated', as the film producer accepted, and it began long before 1943.

John Sweetman

Producer's Preface

The Two Crews

After the Dams Raid its leader Guy Gibson was sent on a propaganda tour of the United States. There he met the Hollywood film producer Howard Hawks, who wanted to make a film about the Dambusters. The film was never made, but a script was sent to the Air Ministry in Whitehall. It is now in the Public Record Office, its margins marked with the scrawled comments of senior RAF officers indignant at the way the Americans had changed the story to suit their creative urges.

For years this has been the case with the Dams Raid, which, along with the Battle of Britain, is the RAF's most famous wartime exploit. And as John Sweetman has noted, even today it is difficult to break away from the myths and misconceptions about the Raid promulgated by the 1955 film *The Dam Busters* (due to necessary oversimplification) and Guy Gibson's book *Enemy Coast Ahead* (due to official vetting).

Since then the story has been retold many times. Television has a tendency to repeat itself – not just literally but by revisiting the same popular stories again and again. The attraction of the Channel 4 Dambusters project therefore was not just the story itself, which is no less gripping than it ever was, but the challenge of telling it in a new and refreshing way – showing in detail just how incredibly complex the raid was for everyone involved.

The first decision we made was to base our telling around just one of Guy Gibson's crews: that of AJ-N for Nan. The crew of AJ-N breached the Eder Dam and flew in one of the eleven of the nineteen aircraft to make it home. Their skipper, Pilot Officer Les Knight, was the second youngest member of his crew but respected by all of them, and three were happily still alive in 2002 to tell his and their stories. An Australian from Victoria, Les did not fit the cliché of brash Australians serving with Bomber Command. He was strong and decisive yet quiet and calm, religious and teetotal. Back home he had taught in Sunday School and was studying to become an accountant. After the raid he was awarded the Distinguished Service Order for his exceptional flying skills and leadership. Sadly he was killed a few weeks later on 617 Squadron's disastrous second low-level mission. Lost in fog attempting to bomb the Dortmund-Ems Canal, Les hit a tree. But he kept his badly damaged aircraft flying long enough for his crew to escape; in other words, he sacrificed himself – as all of the aircrew who flew on the Dams Raid itself had been prepared to. These were some of the reasons that convinced us that AJ-N and its crew should be the focus for our story.

The second decision we made was to try to communicate to an audience as forcefully as we could the intensity of a six-hour mission flown at night at an average height of 100 feet. History has been described as a dialogue between the past and the present, and we wanted to show modern aircrew experiencing some of what Les Knight's crew experienced sixty years ago. To achieve this a simulator was built around an ergonomic Lancaster fuselage in which a new crew could fly the mission again. We are very grateful to the Royal Air Force for lending Channel 4 our eight aircrew and the facilities and expertise to train them in the skills of 1943. We are especially grateful to the new crew themselves for having the courage to share their mistakes and triumphs with a television audience of millions. As a new experiment in historical documentary-making it has been a great success, allowing us to throw light on some aspects of the story in what we hope is an enormously compelling way.

It is very easy for film-makers to be wise after the event from the comfort of an edit suite. For this reason we have been very grateful for the advice and expertise of Dr John Sweetman, who was on hand to ensure that we didn't create any new myths of our own. It is a pleasure to contribute in a small way to his book, which contains much new information from the research for the *Dambusters* programmes for Channel 4.

This project would have been impossible without the wonderful support of former aircrew and groundcrew from 617 Squadron. It has been a privilege to meet them, hear their stories and learn from their experience. When we started on the project there were eleven survivors of the Raid; as I write there are now only eight. Some people believe that they are a dying breed, but perhaps we have shown otherwise.

Gary Johnstone

CHAPTER

1

The RAF at War

Pre-War Hopes and Disappointing Reality

Britain, and especially its air force, had waited a long time for tangible signs of success in the Second World War. In 1940 her army had left the Continent, after which only small, daring Commando raids troubled the enemy on land. At sea, the sinking of the German battleship *Bismarck* in May 1941 had been a morale-booster, but the loss of *Prince of Wales* and *Repulse* off Malaya before that year closed, Axis domination of the Mediterranean, and increasing losses to U-boats in the Atlantic had since been serious set-backs. In 1942 the German warships *Scharnhorst* and *Gneisenau* sailed unimpaired up the Channel from Brest, and *Bismarck*'s sister-ship *Tirpitz* moved menacingly to Norway, where she threatened to attack merchant convoys to the Soviet Union or break out into the Atlantic.

The only means of hitting Germany from Britain was by air. Before hostilities began, hopes were high that bombing would be decisive. The air had added a third dimension to armed conflict during the First World War, and bombers operating from eastern France had attacked the German homeland far beyond the range of front-line artillery. After the Armistice, the CAS, Sir Hugh Trenchard, argued that 'there can be no doubt that we must be prepared for long-distance aerial operations against an enemy's main base of supply'. In other words, his war industry.

During the inter-war years a belief blossomed that bombers would pick out individual factories to destroy, and extreme advocates maintained that they could even win a war by means of a pre-emptive strike without armies or navies getting involved – the so-called 'knock-out blow'. In the 1920s Trenchard convinced ministers that bombers could keep order in rebellious areas like Iraq and the north-west frontier of India at lower cost than the Army. The tactic of 'imperial policing', as this became known, further enhanced the reputation of RAF bombers, and persuaded theorists and staff officers alike that they really could achieve outstanding results in a major conflict.

Imperial policing: the use of bombers to maintain order in Iraq encouraged the belief that 'strategic bombing' would decide future wars.

The statement in 1932 by Cabinet Minister Stanley Baldwin that 'the bomber will always get through' hardly seemed fantastic, therefore. No defence seemed possible against the modern aircraft, with its longer range, large bomb-carrying capacity, defensive gunners and enhanced accuracy of navigation and bombing techniques. An official report declared that on the North-West Frontier RAF bombers could now hit a specific building: 'the house of a sheik'. In the United States it would soon be claimed that its bombers, flying at high altitude, could place their loads 'in a pickle barrel'.

Against this background, as war against Germany became ever more likely, in 1937 the RAF drew up the preparatory Western Air Plans. These were based on the assumption that the bomber would always get through, and that it would accurately locate and attack its designated target. A further assumption was that this could be achieved in daylight by bombers flying in formation with their massed guns providing mutual protection against fighters. One of the Plans estimated that the industrial heartland of Germany (the Ruhr) could be paralysed by flying 3000 sorties in a fortnight to neutralise forty-five prime targets. Such optimism of hitting and rapidly eliminating chosen industrial targets was literally shot down in flames as twin-engine Wellingtons and Blenheims carrying out daylight operations, despite flying in formation, fell victim to German fighters. Switching to night-bombing brought little improvement, mainly due to the shortcomings of navigational aids and target-marking techniques, which became apparent in action. On one occasion, due to a faulty compass, Flight Lieutenant (Flt Lt) G. P. Gibson of 83 Squadron found himself over

Hopes that bombers would crush Germany were dashed when twin-engine aircraft like the Blenheim suffered heavy losses.

Tirpitz anchored behind anti-torpedo nets in Norway, July 1942. Armed with 15-inch guns, the German battleship posed a threat to convoys in the Atlantic and Arctic.

Denmark rather than Norway. In December 1940 photographic reconnaissance showed that attacks by 296 aircraft dropping 262 tons of bombs on two synthetic oil plants at Gelsenkirchen had done no obvious damage. AVM the Hon R. A. Cochrane, later to figure prominently in the dams operation, reflected that 'it was a pity technical developments were not up to pre-war ideas'.

By April 1941 the predicted average night-bombing error of 300 had been raised to 1000 yards. Four months later an Air Ministry study of aerial photographs showed that only one-third of RAF crews credited with successful attacks over Germany actually got within five miles of their targets; in the Ruhr the figure was one in ten (one in fifteen in poor visibility). During the night of 7-8 November 1941, thirty-seven out of 400 bombers were lost. Although 1046 aircraft struck Cologne on 30 May 1942 in the celebrated 'Thousand Bomber Raid', with a 3.8 per cent loss rate, in the period August to October an average of 5.8 per cent of Bomber Command aircraft failed to return from each operation. The creation of a specialised Pathfinder Force to mark targets in advance of the Main Force, and the development of radio aids to navigation such as 'Gee' and 'Oboe', promised more for 1943. By then, however, the Germans had strengthened their air defence, with Major-General Joseph Kammhuber developing a system of co-operation between fighters, radar posts and flak guns, which made even flying in bomber streams at night increasingly hazardous, and reaching and accurately hitting the selected target became even more difficult. Flight Sergeant (F/Sgt) Graham Allen, from Gibson's old 106 Squadron, observed that aircrew were going out 'night after night … worked to death' with no obvious sign of lasting success.

May 1943 threatened to be another bleak month – until the Dambusters Raid. In the words of an RAF intelligence officer, Flt Lt G. E. Pine (a schoolmaster who volunteered for service at the age of 33): 'We did need it.' His sparse words neatly summarised the prevailing atmosphere. In spite of Allied victory in North Africa and German failure to capture Stalingrad or the Caucasus oilfields in the opening months of the year, Axis troops still dominated Europe from the Arctic to the Mediterranean, the Japanese were relentlessly advancing through Burma towards India, and, in the Atlantic, U-boats wolf packs were driving perilous inroads into merchant convoys bringing vital food and supplies to Britain.

The overall picture remained depressing. Pine was right. Something clearly had to be done. But why were German dams chosen?

Germany's Achilles' Heel

Reservoirs and Dams

Dam walls hold back reservoirs, which often contain millions of cubic metres of water. During the First World War, Britain and Germany, fearing that their destruction would cause catastrophic floods in the surrounding area, guarded them against sabotage.

As war again loomed closer in the 1930s, both countries recognised that aerial bombers might do the job more effectively than saboteurs on the ground, so anti-aircraft guns and barrage balloons replaced sentries. At the same time planners came to believe that the prize for destroying a dam was now more valuable than simply local disruption. The dams' reservoirs provided water for critical industrial purposes, like the manufacture of steel, and to amplify drinking supplies for the growing populations of towns and cities. They were important for the production of hydro-electricity and, especially in Germany, could be used to top up the level of canals and rivers (crucial for the movement of war *matériel*).

Devastation of the German war industry was therefore a prime aim of pre-war RAF staff officers, hence their proposal effectively to eliminate the Ruhr armament factories by destroying forty-five power and coking plants. However, a Government committee believed that the same conclusive result could be achieved by attacking just two targets, the Möhne and Sorpe dams, although this task was complicated by the fact that they were different types of structure. The Möhne was a gravity dam, essentially held in place by its own weight; the Sorpe an earth dam, whose central concrete core was supported by two sloping earth ramps. Further east the Eder gravity dam provided critical water supplies for inland waterways connected with the Weser valley.

From October 1937 active steps were taken to achieve destruction of the Ruhr dams in particular, and many Government agencies became involved. The Ordnance Board doubted whether even fifteen 500lb semi-armour piercing (SAP) bombs would

destroy a gravity dam, adding that 'a propelled piercing bomb of high capacity' should be developed. The Germans were thought likely to protect their dams with netting to frustrate torpedo attacks. In March 1938 the Air Staff examined the possibility of using high-explosive (HE) bombs, but from 10-15,000 feet an average error of 102-113 yards could be expected. Under ideal conditions a 6 per cent chance of success existed; in wartime just 2 per cent. Hardly an attractive proposition.

Four months later, the Air Ministry announced that attacking dams and reservoirs must be 'treated as urgent and of pressing importance'. 'Considerable effort' to achieve success was worthwhile because 'not only would power stations automatically be put out of action, but considerable damage would also be caused by the release of floodwater'. This prompted a swift reaction.

A gathering of military and civilian experts under AVM W. Sholto Douglas declared that reservoirs, from which German industrial power was 'almost entirely' derived, were the enemy's 'Achilles' heel'. 'The bulk' of water for the industrial Ruhr came from the Möhne reservoir. Also, by breaching the Möhne Dam the 'low-lying Ruhr Valley would be flooded, so that railways, important bridges, pumping stations and industrial chemical plants would be destroyed or rendered inoperative.' Destruction of 'four or five' other dams would heighten the inevitable chaos.

Learning that a typical gravity dam was 42 feet thick about 40 feet below its crown (figures that would form an integral part of Barnes Wallis's calculations when designing his unique weapon five years later), this meeting on 26 July 1938 went on to review the use of torpedoes fitted with net-cutters, general-purpose (GP) bombs possibly with delayed-action fuses, and anti-submarine bombs. Those present were not hopeful of success. Like the Ordnance Board the previous year, this Air Ministry Bombing Committee favoured the development of a propelled weapon, which could achieve greater penetration of the dam wall.

Although two days later the CAS informed the Secretary of State for Air that the practicality of attacking the Ruhr dams with 1000lb bombs was under active consideration, nothing positive emerged for over a year. The possibility of attacking the Möhne with a radio-controlled drone packed with explosives was raised, but abandoned after the fall of France due to its short range. In July 1940 Bomber Command resurrected the proceedings of the 1938 committee in support of attacking the Möhne Dam. Its Commander-in-Chief, ACM Sir Charles Portal, thought success 'by no means impossible' against 'this most vital target', either with a torpedo attack on the water (reservoir) side or, utilising long-delay fuses, a bombing attack on the 'dry side'. Portal proposed taking 'at least twelve' twin-engine Hampden bombers directly from the production line to constitute a special long-range torpedo force for use on the Möhne.

The Air Ministry rejected this plan, pointing out that 'exhaustive study' for an attack on the dam had been already conducted with discouraging results. Messrs Nobel, the armament manufacturers, had made 'an elaborate series of tests' to determine how much explosive would be needed to breach a gravity dam, and the answer was far too

Opposite Above The Möhne Dam, with the power station to the left and the dam wall to the right. Note the two towers and the buttress beyond, where flak guns would be mounted before the raid.

Opposite Below The Eder Dam, with Waldeck Castle in the foreground, over which the Lancasters would dive to attack the dam (middle left).

Air Chief Marshal Sir Charles Portal, whose support for an attack on the Möhne Dam in 1940, as C-in-C Bomber Command, made him sympathetic to Wallis's scheme when he became CAS three years later.

much. It might be feasible to drop a hundred or more mines against the water face of the dam and countermine them with an HE bomb, 'but the practical difficulties of this method are considered to be insuperable'. In truth, another depressing conclusion.

However, an in-depth study of the problem was already being conducted on behalf of the Technical Branch (Armament) of the Ministry of Supply research department at Shrewsbury. In May 1940 an experienced First World War veteran holding the position of assistant superintendent, Wing Commander (Wg Cdr) C. R. Finch Noyes, had been tasked to re-examine all the existing data on German dams. He produced a preliminary report in September, in which he argued that if 20,000lb of explosive were exploded against the face of a gravity dam 40 feet below its crest 'there seems a probability that the dam would go', making clear that he had the Möhne in mind. He envisaged a 'missile' being launched from an aircraft flying at 80m.p.h. 'very low over the surface of the water' and propelling itself towards the dam wall about a mile away. There it would 'destroy its buoyancy', sink to 40 feet and be detonated by standard hydrostatic fuzes, which would be activated by water pressure at the set depth.

Finch Noyes revealed that he had already carried out preliminary tests with half-scale models at a works in Kingston, Surrey. He was looking at two possible weapons: a hydroplane skimmer, self-propelled and 'directionally stable', which would jump over defensive torpedo nets; or a torpedo 'partly or wholly submerged'. Each of these would have a total weight of 3000lb (including 2000lb of explosive). Two means of propulsion for them were being examined: one involved a 'rocket-under-water plus steam jet', the other a 20mm automatic gun firing blanks astern in a tube running longitudinally through the centre of the explosive container.

These proposals, which were still at a preliminary experimental stage, were discussed with the Vice-President of the Ordnance Board. He showed keen interest but told Finch Noyes that 'a sudden demand' had arisen to attack the Möhne and that an attempt would be made 'with existing weapons' unless something more potent could be quickly developed. Finch Noyes replied that a cordite charge container could be supplied 'at once' by the Ballistic Department at Woolwich. A Wellington could carry two of the proposed 3000lb missiles, one slung under each wing, and ten of these bombers could thus transport 40,000lb of explosive to be detonated against the wall of the dam at short intervals.

In his report, Finch Noyes outlined further details of his recommended mode of attack. The weapon would be released at a predetermined height above the water by each aircraft. That height would be judged by a cup or weight attached to a trailing wire of suitable length. Furthermore, the missile would have to be robust enough to withstand striking the water at 80m.p.h. from 50 feet.

During the winter of 1940–1 Finch Noyes refined his work, which he summarised in April 1941. He now proposed an attack on the Möhne Dam in moonlight by sixteen Wellingtons carrying a total of 64,000lb of explosive, which would allow for losses or mechanical failure. The attacking aircraft were to glide from 20,000 to 5500 feet at right angles to the dam wall and reach the lower height 5½ miles from it, releasing the weapons so that they struck the water half a mile from the target. Finch Noyes explained that the torpedo or skimmer – both versions were evidently still under consideration – would travel a horizontal mile for every 1000 feet of altitude on release. When the weapon hit the water, cordite charges would ignite and propel it towards the wall where it would strike, sink to 40 feet and explode. Finch Noyes reiterated that 'the destruction of the Möhne Dam would flood the Ruhr Valley and disorganise its industry. It is probably very heavily defended, so it is desirable to attack it from a distance and from a height.' His proposed tactic would, he maintained, secure success and protect the aircraft, which would be able to turn away well short of the dam.

Senior staff officers were sceptical, to say the least. They believed that a torpedo travelling at 40 knots would bounce back after hitting the wall, not sink 'in a docile manner' beside it. Destruction of the Möhne would undoubtedly 'paralyse' the Ruhr industry and had been 'considered on many occasions'. But all previous schemes had been abandoned because of the 'enormous quantity of explosive' needed for success. Finch Noyes's latest proposal did not solve the problem of delivering the necessary amount to the dam wall. 'Once we use a gliding weapon all sorts of errors in ranging and in line arise immediately, and are added to enormously when wind has to be taken into account.' Finch Noyes's proposal was therefore rejected.

Nevertheless, at the close of 1941 the Möhne Dam and other western German dams remained priority targets. Though at the time unrecognised, Finch Noyes had made an important contribution to the search for a means of destroying them, with his proposal that a special squadron should release a new weapon at low level to travel across the surface of a reservoir and strike the dam wall. Almost another eighteen months would elapse before Wallis would design and perfect his weapon to breach the Möhne, which would reflect aspects of Finch Noyes's plan.

Scientific Challenge

Enter Barnes Wallis

Barnes Neville Wallis. His agile mind produced countless ideas to aid the war effort, of which the dams weapon was only one.

The spring of 1942 was decisive in the search for a way to destroy the German dams. Barnes Neville Wallis, the 54-year-old Assistant Chief Designer (Structures) at Vickers-Armstrongs' works in Weybridge, had long been associated with the aeronautical industry. Originally trained as a marine engineer, in 1913 he had joined the Vickers Airship Department, in which he worked during the First World War. In 1916 at Barrow he met a young Royal Naval Air Service officer, the Hon R. A. Cochrane. That encounter and their subsequent friendship would be important in the run-up to the Dambusters Raid almost thirty years later. When set-backs occurred during the development of the 'bouncing bomb', Cochrane never lost faith in Wallis. 'If Wally said he'd do it, he would.'

Until 1930 Wallis remained closely involved in the design and construction of airships, culminating in the R100. Subsequently he concentrated on military aeroplanes such as the Wellesley and Wellington. After the outbreak of war in 1939 his fertile mind dreamed up a variety of ingenious schemes to aid the war effort, such as an aerial method of neutralising magnetic mines at sea.

Quite independently Wallis began to gather information about vulnerable targets in Germany, including dams and particularly the Möhne. He believed that a 22,400lb (10-ton) bomb containing

7 tons of explosive could be dropped from 40,000 feet to penetrate the earth or water beside the target, burrow beneath the ground and explode so that the dam collapsed. Because no existing aircraft could carry such a bomb, Wallis designed a six-engine Victory bomber capable of 330m.p.h. at 35,000 feet and with a range of 4000 miles. He enlisted the help of the MAP, then housed in Imperial Chemical Industries' headquarters in Millbank, which in turn authorised the Road Research Laboratory (RRL) at Harmondsworth and the Building Research Station at Garston to construct 1:50 scale models of the Möhne. Small explosive charges, representing scaled-down versions of his intended bomb, were detonated at a distance from these – with disappointing results. It proved impossible to predict that even a 10-ton bomb dropped close to the dam would breach it, and production of the monster bomber, with a wingspan of 160 feet, an all-up weight of 107,000lb, and needing a minimum 1200 yards to take off, did not proceed.

Wallis refused to give up. He knew that destruction of the Möhne Dam ranked high in Air Staff priorities and he had already been given much encouragement and, crucially, information from official sources including the MAP and Air Ministry. He was not, however, apparently aware of Finch Noyes's proposal to explode a weapon in contact with the dam wall, or perhaps he did not consider it possible. A. R. (Dick) Collins, the scientific officer in charge of tests on the models at Harmondsworth, gave the necessary impetus to this line of thought when, unofficially, in February 1942 he detonated one of the scaled-down charges against the face of a model with a spectacular

A. R. (Dick) Collins, the scientific officer at the Road Research Laboratory responsible for tests on models at Harmondsworth and Garston, and on the Nant-y-Gro Dam in Wales.

result. The wall shattered. Curiously, because of these experiments Collins and his assistants became known at the RRL as 'the Dam Blasters'.

By now, too, another experimental dimension had entered the equation. While the tests into the viability of the 10-ton bomb were in progress, the disused Nant-y-Gro Dam near Rhayader in Wales, one-fifth the size of the Möhne Dam, was provisionally acquired for upgraded trials. To produce the same results as those for the 1:50 scale models of the Möhne, 1:10 models of the Nant-y-Gro were constructed at Harmondsworth. On 1 May 1942 Collins conducted a test on the Nant-y-Gro Dam itself in Wallis's presence and conclusively proved that a charge of no less than 30,000lb would be needed if dropped at a distance from the Möhne Dam. A contact explosion was the only option.

Years after the event, Wallis wrote to Collins explaining that 'the bouncing bomb was originated solely to meet the requirement so convincingly demonstrated by your experiments that actual contact with the masonry of the dam was essential.' In the spring of 1942 Wallis found a way of achieving this accuracy. He would bounce a specially developed weapon across the surface of the reservoir. Wallis later recalled: 'Early in 1942 I had the idea of a missile, which if dropped on the water at a considerable distance upstream of the dam would reach the dam in a series of ricochets, and after impact against the dam would sink in close contact with the upstream face of the masonry.' He could not explain precisely how or when this occurred to him, but it had no direct link with children skimming pebbles across water. (This involved revolution around a vertical axis, whereas Wallis's weapon would revolve around the horizontal.) Nor was he inspired by reports that Nelson's gunners had bounced round shot off the waves to increase the range of their artillery. Only after settling on his method did he discover this.

By the beginning of April Wallis was ready to begin simple experiments on the patio of his house at Effingham in Surrey, by projecting a supply of his daughter Elisabeth's marbles on to the surface of water in a tin bath balanced on a table. He was seeking a Law of Ricochet to guarantee consistency of bounce. Towards the end of the month Wallis conducted more experiments using a catapult to fire spherical and oblong shapes across the surface of Silvermere Lake near Weybridge, deciding on the strength of these that his new weapon should be spherical. This was less satisfactory than an oblong for ricocheting, but he judged it more suitable for aerial bombing.

In mid-May Wallis outlined his notion in a paper entitled 'Spherical Bomb – Surface Torpedo'. He explained that, when dropped, the angle of incidence must not exceed 7 degrees otherwise the sphere would sink. 'By approaching the target in a fast glide and flattening out, the bomb should be dropped from a height not greater than 26 feet when travelling at a speed of 470ft/sec.' He calculated that if released 3500 feet from the dam wall, the proposed weapon would bounce five times: the first to half the altitude of the aircraft on release, decreasing to the last of just 4 feet. He recommended 'a double skin', bridged by 'a series of light timber beams or roughly welded steel girders' for the weapon, so that its density could be varied during the experimental process.

Possibly to protect the originality of the concept, Wallis left one critical element out of this document – back-spin. This he later explained would be necessary to ensure that the weapon did not sink on impact with the water, would make direct progress towards the target without drifting off line and, absolutely critically, would not bounce back after striking the dam wall. Instead it would crawl down the side of it to explode 30 feet below the waterline.

The third phase of the bouncing bomb experiments occurred at the National Physical Laboratory at Teddington, which housed two large indoor water tanks. Between June and September 1942 Wallis conducted a series of tests mainly in the No. 2 tank, which was 640 feet long, 23 feet wide and 9 feet deep. Across it his Vickers-Armstrongs' staff fired 2-inch-diameter spheres made of different materials such as lead and balsa-wood in the search for the elusive Law of Ricochet. To discover how the weapon would behave once it struck the target, a sheet of steel was positioned in the

Left The 1:50 scale model of the Möhne Dam at the Building Research Station, Garston. It comprised three million individual blocks, and was used for tests during the winter of 1940-1.

Below The 1:10 model of the Nant-y-Gro Dam (itself 1:5 of the Möhne) at the Road Research Laboratory, Harmondsworth, on which scaled-down tests were carried out. Early in 1942 Collins successfully detonated a charge in contact with it.

Opposite Nant-y-Gro Dam, 1 May 1942: a failed attempt at destruction with a charge detonated at a distance from it. This sequence was filmed by Dick Collins.

Below Sir Henry Tizard, scientific adviser to the Air Ministry, who coined the term 'bouncing bomb'. Wallis found him 'pleasant' and 'always supportive'.

water. Two rectangular galvanised cisterns, open at the top and each fitted with small windows, were loaded with cast iron ballast and lowered into the water on both sides of the tank adjacent to the metal sheet. Lights were fitted in one of the cisterns, while a photographer using a ciné camera occupied the other.

A series of influential military and civilian visitors made the trek from their London offices to witness the experiments, and Sir Henry Tizard (scientific adviser to the Air Ministry) soon reacted positively: 'It looks very promising … I certainly think now that a full-scale test is desirable with a Wellington.' On 25 June permission to do so was granted. At this stage Wallis planned a final weapon about 7ft. 6in. in diameter, but agreed that to extrapolate the results of the 2-inch-ball tests at Teddington would be 'beyond the bounds of reason'. Conversion of a Wellington to carry a sphere 4ft. 6in. in diameter would provide invaluable intermediate data.

Meanwhile, at the Road Research Laboratory Collins set about arranging a second test at the Nant-y-Gro Dam, this time with a contact explosive to validate the results

of similar experiments with 2oz charges on the models at Harmondsworth. On 14 July 1942, therefore, a 500lb anti-submarine mine (containing 279lb of explosive) was positioned by means of scaffolding at the mid-point of the disused dam, 7ft. 6in. from its crest and in contact with the face. At 1700 the charge was detonated. A cauldron of bubbling water in the reservoir was drawn upwards in a huge spout so sensational that Collins, who was filming the event, momentarily took his finger off the camera button. When the spray cleared, spectators saw that a hole had been punched in the centre of the dam. Collins calculated that a charge of approximately 7500lb exploded 30 feet below the surface of the reservoir in contact with the wall would cause a 50-feet-deep breach in the Möhne Dam, through which 70 per cent of the reservoir's contents would escape. Later Collins reflected on the pivotal nature of this experiment: 'If this test had failed, and the [Welsh] dam had been severely damaged but not breached, the case for an attack would have been seriously

weakened.' Without the work of the Road Research Laboratory, which Wallis did not in any way direct or control, the Dambusters Raid would never have been launched. Wallis acknowledged the commitment of its staff and the active encouragement of its director, Dr W. H. Glanville, when he said to Collins: 'I can't tell you what to do, you're telling me.'

Despite the considerable support that Wallis was undoubtedly receiving from several official sources, opposition to his extraordinary plan to destroy the German dams remained considerable. Shortly before the second Nant-y-Gro test in July 1942, the Director of Scientific Research (DSR) at the MAP wrote disdainfully: 'I think we can safely say that the gravity dam is a hopeless proposition.' On 29 September Wallis met Winston Churchill's scientific adviser and recorded: 'I see Lord Cherwell and find him very unresponsive … [he] doubted if the Dams were of any consequence.' Tizard, however, remained a firm supporter, writing the very next day about the use of an '8000lb charge': 'I should myself be inclined to advise that Wallis be instructed straight away to submit an opinion as to whether a bouncing bomb of this size could be fitted to a Stirling or a Lancaster.' This was the first use of the now familiar term 'bouncing bomb'.

Confusingly, Wallis continued to receive mixed signals. The Air Attack on Dams Committee, which had originally been created to consider his 10-ton bomb proposal, gave him no specific encouragement at its meeting on 12 October. Yet a different conference at the Institution of Mechanical Engineers on 16 November, which was

Captain Joseph 'Mutt' Summers (Vickers-Armstrongs' chief test pilot)

attended by representatives of the experimental staff at Shrewsbury (Finch Noyes's base), the MAP and Woolwich Arsenal, revealed that detonation of a new underwater explosive (Torpex) had been carried out in connection with Wallis's proposed weapon and appropriate tests would continue.

Parallel to all of this, Wallis had been making use of the modified Wellington authorised in July. On 20 October a special rig had been installed in the fuselage for spinning tests with the 4ft. 6in.-diameter practice weapon on the ground at Weybridge. Following other similar tests, on 20 October Captain Joseph 'Mutt' Summers (Vickers-Armstrongs' chief test pilot) took the Wellington into the air over the Queen Mary Reservoir close by, and Wallis spun four of the spheres simultaneously by means of a device using the hydraulic system that operated the bomb-bay doors. Summers detected no discernible difference in the handling of the aircraft, and Wallis was relieved that spinning in the air caused no gyroscopic effect. Several of those who took his full-size weapon to the dams would disagree on the night.

For the moment, though, Wallis was satisfied, and he secured permission to proceed to the next series of tests.

On 4 December, with Wallis acting as bomb-aimer and another Vickers' test pilot, R. C. (Bob) Handasyde, also on board, Summers took off from Weybridge in the Wellington for the First Trial at a stretch of water between the Chesil Beach spit and the mainland close to Weymouth. Unfortunately the welded spheres burst on impact. Wallis was not deterred. He ordered the outer casings to be re-inforced with a mixture of granulated cork and cement for another try.

The Second Trial at Chesil Beach took place on 15 December, with a camera in the Wellington and another on the ground to record the results. This time Summers flew from the grass runway of RAF Warmwell just to the north, with Handasyde again occupying the second pilot's seat. Wallis opted to observe the proceedings on the ground at the test site. Summers dived at top speed to release two spheres from 60 feet. Both apparently shattered on impact, but after rowing around for two hours Wallis recovered one from 5 feet of icy water. It was damaged, but not broken. If strengthened, there was every prospect of success.

Captain R. C. (Bob) Handasyde, Vickers-Armstrongs' test pilot, was closely involved at Chesil Beach and made several drops off Reculver.

During the Third Trial on 10 January 1943, to Wallis's delight a sphere 'did one enormous leap to a height of 55 feet'. On 23 January a wooden-cased sphere was used and bounced thirteen times. Two days later, during the Fourth Trial, another wooden sphere bounced '20-22' times. Further tests on 5 February confirmed these results. One sphere travelled 1315 yards, almost twice the distance predicted in the model tests. Wallis was now certain that his concept would work. The German dams could be breached with a bouncing bomb.

He summarised his findings in a nineteen-page document entitled 'Air Attack on Dams', complete with explanatory diagrams, tables, footnotes and illustrations. Following the Nant-y-Gro tests, he was confident that a 6500lb charge (not Collins's 7500lb charge predicted in July 1942) exploded in contact with the face of the masonry wall 30 feet below the surface of the water could breach 'the largest gravity dams in Germany'. The overall weight of the bomb, including the casing, would be well within the carrying capacity of a Lancaster bomber. He then turned to the Sorpe Dam, with its different construction, which would be 'practically self-destroying if a substantial leak can be established within the water-tight core'; in other words, if the central concrete wall could be cracked. He believed that success would result if detonation occurred on the water side of the dam 'at a suitable distance below the surface'. To achieve this, aircraft would approach at right angles to the dam, as at all of the others, and release the weapon 'at extreme range' so that it would reach the sloping face as its momentum was spent. Then 'it would drop back into the water rather than leap over the crest'. When it exploded 30 feet underwater, sufficient force would be transmitted through the earth support to cause a fracture in the core, which would gradually widen as water seeped through, bringing about collapse of the structure.

Wallis listed five dams (the Möhne, Sorpe, Lister, Ennepe and Henne) that together held back 254 million cubic metres of water to supply the 'domestic and industrial' needs of 'the Ruhr district'. He argued that the emptying of the Möhne reservoir alone would 'cause a disaster of the first magnitude' and that the destruction of the others would enhance the disruption of traffic on the Ruhr River and possibly the Dortmund-Ems Canal. Floods would damage factories, road and rail systems as well as thirteen electricity stations in the area. Further east, the Eder and Diemel dams held back 222 million cubic metres of water, their principal function being to 'provide a regular supply of water for pumping from the Weser [River] into the Mittelland Canal', a 200-mile-long lateral link running from the Rhine to Berlin and transporting crucial industrial products. Flooding would affect factories in towns like Kassel, inundate and wash away valuable agricultural soil, and destroy important electricity generating stations. Much of this was a repetition of information already contained in previous staff papers, but that at least ensured a sympathetic hearing.

Not from every quarter, however. Harris, whose Bomber Command would have to execute any attack on the dams, reacted badly. On 14 February, referring to the details of Wallis's proposal and the possibility of losing a valuable Lancaster squadron from his bombing campaign on Germany for 'two or three weeks', he wrote: 'This is tripe of the wildest description. There are so many ifs & ands that there is not the smallest chance of its working.' Unless the bomb were '*perfectly*' balanced the vibration as it spun would either 'wreck' the aircraft or 'tear the bomb loose'. 'I don't believe a word of its supposed ballistics on the surface... The war will be over before it works – & it never will.' He was utterly opposed to 'putting aside Lancasters & reducing our bombing effort on this wild goose chase.' Four days later, in a personal note, he sought the CAS's support against 'all sorts of enthusiasts and panacea mongers now careering round the MAP suggesting the taking of about 30 Lancasters off the production line to rig them up for this weapon, when the weapon itself exists so far only within the imagination of those who conceived it.' Harris thought Wallis's idea 'just about the maddest proposition as a weapon that we have yet come across – and that is saying something.' 'I am prepared to bet my shirt (a) that the weapon itself cannot be passed a prototype for trial inside six months; (b) that its ballistics will in no way resemble those claimed for it; (c) that it will be impossible to keep such a weapon in adequate balance either when rotating it prior to release or at all in storage; and (d) that it will not work, when we have got it.' He ended by reminding the CAS that attempts to use heavy bombers in low-level attacks had 'almost without exception been costly failures'.

Harris had a point. Wallis's weapon had not yet been finalised, and Harris retained a healthy suspicion of eccentric inventors from his First World War days in the Royal Flying Corps, during which he had reacted scathingly to a suggestion that he fire a harpoon at Zeppelins over London, pointing out that as the gas-filled envelope exploded his aircraft would just have reached its vicinity. Crackpot schemes during the present conflict such as dropping rats with incendiaries tied to their tails to set fire to the Black Forest in south-west Germany scarcely improved his opinion.

When Wallis travelled to High Wycombe in company with Summers, the test pilot, to show Harris films of the various airborne tests, he was predictably greeted with an unwelcoming roar: 'What the hell do you damned inventors want? My boys' lives are too precious to be thrown away by you.' Even after seeing the films Harris remained

Air Chief Marshal Sir Arthur Harris. As C-in-C Bomber Command, he dismissed Wallis's proposal as 'tripe'. Overruled by the CAS, he eventually declared that the engineer could sell him 'a pink elephant'.

hostile, and with good reason, as Cochrane now Air Officer Commanding (AOC) No. 5 Bomber Group, who would eventually oversee the Dambusters Raid) remarked. Wallis was proposing to project 'a five-ton lump of iron across a lake'. And Harris's operational problems, given the continuing loss rate of his bombers, were certainly acute. The forecast production of new Lancasters for April 1943 was 123. Wallis's supporters wanted a quarter of this monthly total for one, to Harris's mind bizarre, operation.

On 23 February Wallis received a shock. Summoned to Vickers-Armstrongs' main office in London, he was instructed by the company's Chairman, Sir Charles Craven, to 'stop this silly nonsense about the destruction of the dams'. He was making a thorough nuisance of himself at the MAP, upsetting members of the Air Staff, and directly or indirectly damaging the firm's commercial interests. Utterly shocked, Wallis offered to resign, to which Craven reacted violently, banging the desk and shouting 'Mutiny!'. Suspecting that Craven had been surreptitiously approached, Wallis wrote in his diary: 'What happened on the Golf Links at Ulverston?'

Unknown to Wallis, or Craven, events elsewhere were moving much more favourably, an indication of the bureaucratic maze at the centre of the decision-making process. The proverbial right and left hands really did not know what the other was

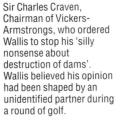

Sir Charles Craven, Chairman of Vickers-Armstrongs, who ordered Wallis to stop his 'silly nonsense about destruction of dams'. Wallis believed his opinion had been shaped by an unidentified partner during a round of golf.

doing. The CAS in 1943 was ACM Sir Charles Portal, who, while holding Harris's current post in 1940, had proposed sending a special squadron of Hampdens armed with torpedoes against the Möhne. He therefore proved rather less critical than Harris had hoped. Replying to Harris's personal plea, he refused to dismiss Wallis's plan out of hand and revealed that he had authorised the allocation of three Lancasters for trial purposes. He assured Harris that he would not allow more of 'your precious Lancasters to be diverted' until the concept of the new weapon had been fully tested. The unpalatable implication from Harris's viewpoint was that, if these trials were successful, Portal would back the proposed operation. Shortly afterwards he told Harris: 'If you want to win the war, bust the dams.'

Three days after his traumatic encounter with Craven, Wallis experienced a complete reversal of fortunes. Called to a meeting at the MAP on 26 February, he not only learned that the operation was to go ahead after all, but that Portal wanted 'every endeavour' to carry it out that spring. The Möhne reservoir would soon be full and the Germans would begin withdrawing water from it at a rate of 10 feet per month. Because Wallis's weapon would not be effective if exploded lower than 40 feet below the crest, the operation had to be launched by 26 May at the latest.

Wallis had often forecast that only eight weeks would be needed to develop 'Upkeep' (the codename allocated to his back-spun weapon). He later confessed that as he left the meeting he felt 'physically sick, because somebody had called my bluff'. He realised 'the terrible responsibility of making good all my claims.' For, in spite of Wallis's enthusiasm and optimism, on 26 February no full-size weapon had been tested and, in truth, none was even on the drawing-board.

Norbert Rowe, a long-standing friend and present at the meeting, sensed Wallis's anguish. Knowing that Wallis had 'spiritual depths', he offered him a copy of a prayer to St Joseph, which Rowe found helpful in times of stress. Faith, in every sense of the word, was a much-needed commodity now.

Special Formation

No. 617 Squadron Created

Air Vice-Marshal the Hon. R. A. Cochrane, Air Officer Commanding No. 5 Bomber Group, of which 617 Squadron was part.

Once the decision had been taken to back Wallis's weapon, operational plans to use it against the dams became an RAF priority. On 15 March the C-in-C Bomber Command, Harris, gave that responsibility to No. 5 Bomber Group, whose AOC, Cochrane, was ordered to form a new squadron without reducing his Main Force effort. Ideally, it would come from volunteer crews that had completed, or nearly completed, at least one tour of thirty operations. Harris nominated as the Squadron Commander 24-year-old Acting Wg Cdr Guy Penrose Gibson DSO DFC and Bar, who was unknown to Cochrane but who had served under Harris when he commanded 5 Group.

That day Gibson was preparing to relinquish command of 106 Bomber Squadron at Syerston, officially after a total of forty-two sorties in Hampdens, ninety-nine as a night-fighter pilot with Beaufighters, and twenty-nine further bomber operations flying the twin-engine Manchester or its four-engine successor, the Lancaster. However, his rear gunner on 106 Squadron was convinced that he did not enter in his log book every operation that he flew. He was a short, energetic man, one that, as a gunner on 617 Squadron remarked, not everybody 'dearly loved'. Variously described by those serving under him as 'arrogant', 'cocky' or 'a hard nut', without doubt he had a strong personality. Suddenly, instead of a well-earned leave, he was posted to 5 Group

Left Squadron Commander: Guy Gibson with members of 106 Squadron, which he commanded before 617 Squadron.

Below Gibson wearing a German 'Mae West' taken from a shot-down pilot.

Group Captain J. N. H. 'Charles' Whitworth, Station Commander at RAF Scampton and Gibson's immediate superior.

Flight Sergeant L. J. Sumpter, a Grenadier guardsman, who volunteered for aircrew. He was awarded the DFM as bomb-aimer in Shannon's Lancaster, which attacked the Eder Dam.

Headquarters at Grantham and told to write a book about his wartime experiences. On his third day there Cochrane asked him to do one more sortie. Gibson agreed, and the very next day (19 March) discovered a little about the task ahead. He would command a new squadron based at RAF Scampton, whose station commander was Group Captain (Gp Capt) J. N. H. 'Charles' Whitworth, and which currently housed only 57 Squadron. Cochrane revealed that the mysterious operation would not be carried out for about two months, and that Gibson must ensure that his crews, when they eventually arrived, were proficient in low flying at night.

Squadron X, Gibson's new charge, had nominally been created on 17 March, when AVM R. D. Oxland, Senior Air Staff Officer (SASO) at Bomber Command, described details of 'Upkeep' to Cochrane, and revealed that it would be used 'in the first instance' against the Möhne Dam. That operation 'will not, it is thought, prove particularly dangerous, but it will undoubtedly require skilled crews'. Hence the accent on experience.

Later the impression would arise that Gibson personally chose all the aircrew members of his new squadron, and that most of them were young, highly decorated and boisterous. He undoubtedly did choose some, but certainly not all. Of the 133 who would fly to the dams, 103 were not decorated, and many were relatively inexperienced: F/Sgt L. J. Sumpter (Shannon's bomb-aimer) had completed only thirteen operations, Sgt D. P. Heal (Brown's navigator) seven. In theory twenty-one complete crews would be at Scampton by 31 March, but in reality they assembled more haphazardly. Flt Lt D. J. Shannon DFC RAAF, a twenty-year-old pilot, reached the squadron indirectly: he had been posted from 106 Squadron to the Pathfinders, but seized the opportunity to rejoin Gibson, although only his navigator agreed to go with him. At Scampton he acquired a bomb-aimer and flight engineer who approached him from 57 Squadron because their pilot had been grounded for medical reasons. Two unattached gunners were added, but Shannon ('baby face, but an ace pilot,' according to the Squadron Adjutant) did not get a permanent wireless operator until 20 April. Although he certainly did look youthful,

Shannon had a wealth of experience and easily commanded the respect of his crew. Flt Lt J. V. Hopgood DFC, who had taken Gibson up to familiarise him with flying a Lancaster instead of the Manchester, and F/Sgt – soon promoted to Pilot Officer (Plt Off) – L. J. Burpee DFM RCAF also came from 106 Squadron and were, like Shannon, undoubtedly selected by Gibson. However, 57 Squadron had just been increased to three flights, and four crews from the third was simply posted across the station: Sqn Ldr H. M. Young DFC, Flt Lt W. Astell DFC, Plt Off G. Rice, and Sergeant (Sgt) Lovell – not all willingly. Rice vainly protested at the transfer. Similarly, Sgt S. Oancia, bomb-aimer in F/Sgt K. W. Brown RCAF's crew from 44 Squadron, arrived at Scampton on 30 March and mused that 'I do not recall volunteering for this transfer'. The flight engineer (Sgt B. Feneron) had vainly voiced his protest when told of the transfer. Brown's all-NCO crew had not completed one operational tour over the Continent.

Flight Lieutenant D. J. Shannon DFC RAAF, pilot of AJ-L on the Dams Raid, for which he was awarded the DSO.

Three crews were supplied by 97 Squadron, piloted by the New Zealander Flt Lt J. L. Munro, Flt Lt D. H. Maltby DFC and Flt Lt J. C. McCarthy RCAF (an American who wore dual shoulder flashes 'USA' and 'Canada'). McCarthy was one of those approached personally by Gibson, and his crew agreed to go to the new squadron. However, there was a snag. Sgt G. L. Johnson, the bomb-aimer, was due to get married and his future wife declared, 'If you're not here on 3 April, don't bother to come at all.' So, to Johnson's relief, 'The crew went up to Gibson with Joe in the lead, and he said, "We've finished our tour, we're entitled to our leave, our bomb-aimer's getting married." And we got four days leave.' McCarthy was larger than life in many ways. 'Six feet plus, as broad almost as he was high, and hands like hams. A great sense of humour and in my book a brilliant pilot,' Johnson explained. He had a prolific capacity for alcohol, which never seemed to affect him. One hardened drinker challenged him to a drinking contest in the Scampton mess. When that unfortunate optimist collapsed, his conqueror carried him to bed. McCarthy was outspoken, as the episode concerning Johnson's wedding showed. 'He expected everybody to do their job properly, and if they didn't he let them know in no uncertain terms.' McCarthy's rear gunner, Flying Officer (Fg Off) D. Rodger, 'could make anybody laugh, absolutely anybody, he had a wonderful sense of humour,' Johnson thought. On operations, 'when tension began to drift a little bit, he could come up with the driest of comments over the intercom. Very much the life and soul of the crew.'

Munro had flown 21 operations with his crew, but one of his gunners and the bomb-aimer opted not to go to Scampton. He therefore asked Harry Weeks RCAF and

Flight Lieutenant J. C. McCarthy (far right), an American pilot serving in the RCAF, with his crew – from left to right, Radcliffe, Johnson, Batson, Eaton and MacLean – when with 97 Squadron. McCarthy was awarded the DSO after the Dams Raid.

Jim H. Clay to join him from 97 Squadron for something that would be 'probably special, probably dangerous'. They agreed and soon fitted in. Clay recalled that Munro was 'a tall New Zealander, somewhat dour, so we christened him "Happy Munro". He was a first-class pilot and besides didn't object when we raided his hoard of parcels from home.' Whittaker (Martin's flight engineer) agreed that Munro was 'tall, efficient and commanded respect'.

With their crews, Fg Off R. N. G. Barlow DFC RAAF arrived from 61 Squadron, and Sgt C. T. Anderson and Sgt W. C. Townsend DFM from 49 Squadron. Barlow would be promoted Flt Lt before the Dams Raid; Anderson and Townsend to F/Sgt Townsend's crew had just completed a tour of operations and the wireless operator chose not to come. At Scampton F/Sgt G. Chalmers took his place – by accident. He wanted an NCO crew, none of whom knew (least of all Howard himself) that the Australian navigator Lance Howard had been commissioned in January. The stately pace of Service bureaucracy could not be quickened even in wartime.

Plt Off W. H. T. Ottley DFC did not reach Scampton with his crew from 207 Squadron until 6 April, having volunteered to join Gibson, whom he knew, on hearing about the new squadron. Gibson rang Flt Lt H. B. M. 'Mick' Martin DFC at 1654 Heavy Conversion Unit, inviting him 'to come to the party'. Martin – with a reputation for skilful low-flying and, according to Grayston, Knight's flight engineer,

Flight Lieutenants
J.L. Munro and J.F. Leggo,
Section Officer Fay Gillan
and Flight Lieutenant
H.B. Martin. Leggo was
Martin's navigator; Gillan
was an Intelligence Officer
attached to 617 Squadron.

'absolutely brilliant, he'd fly the Lancaster like a fighter' – put together a crew and joined Squadron X on 31 March. From 50 Squadron came Sqn Ldr H. E. Maudslay DFC and twenty-two year-old Plt Off L. G. Knight RAAF with their crews. The Australian wireless operator, Sgt R. Kellow, described how Knight's crew finished at Scampton. 'The offer presented to us sounded interesting and with our faith in each member's ability, we made up our minds there and then that we would accept the offer and move across as a crew to this new squadron.' This crew, like others, had been chosen because of its bombing record.

Knight had interrupted his accountancy studies to volunteer for the RAAF. One of his gunners, Sgt F. E. Sutherland, later paid a generous tribute to him: 'He was short but very muscular, strong in the shoulders and arms. He was a wonderful pilot. He didn't smoke or drink and he was an example to all of us. He was a good disciplinarian. He was very quiet, but if you were out of line he quietly told us that you know you'd better not do that again. So we didn't. We respected and admired him. He was just a wonderful person.' Grayston, the flight engineer, agreed. Knight was 'a very quiet sort of individual. He never issued a harsh word really, apart from telling everybody to shut up because they were all talking at the same time on the R/T [radio-telephony]. Very calm, collected, never known him to alter at any time even when you were in the worst predicament.' Grayston thought him a 'brilliant' pilot. Sgt H. E. O'Brien, the rear gunner, believed Knight 'the coolest and quickest thinking person I have ever met. And, in my opinion, the most knowledgeable person on the squadron with respect to his job.'

The pilot and gunners of AJ-N: (left to right) Sergeant F. E. Sutherland RCAF, Pilot Officer L. G. Knight RAAF (pilot), and Sergeant H. E. O'Brien RCAF.

When the crew originally came together, Knight was not commissioned, but when 'he got to be an officer, he would come over and visit us in the Sergeants' Mess' to make sure that the NCOs still felt part of one crew. They did, though, tend to take a minor liberty with him on these occasions. O'Brien explained that because Knight neither drank nor smoked, 'he always had money for a beer or so, when we reminded him it was his turn every other round.' Knight is unlikely to have been fooled. Fg Off H. S. Hobday and Fg Off E. C. Johnson, both 31 and 'the elder statesmen', echoed Sutherland's remarks. Like him, they highly regarded the young pilot. Sutherland, who hotly denied that his nickname 'Doc' stemmed from the time he operated on the family cat, and the other Canadian gunner, O'Brien ('a great big guy, weighing about 210lb' and, because of his size, unable to wear the harness to which his parachute could be clipped in his turret), admitted that as unattached youngsters they were rather wild. Sutherland recalled: 'He and I had a reputation for being the sloppiest guys on the squadron.' Despite their nocturnal revelries, they never reported unfit for duty. The 'good influence' on them of the older members of the crew was marked – 'they were stable, they'd matured'. 'If we got in any difficulties we'd go and talk to Johnny. He was always helpful like a father figure.'

F/Sgt (soon Plt Off) V. W. Byers RCAF, Flt Lt H. S. Wilson and F/Sgt G. Lanchester RCAF and their crews also converged on Scampton. Gibson's crew, contrary to the cinema portrayal, did not, except for the navigator, come with him from 106 Squadron, and he formed his at Scampton from unattached aircrew. Eventually Squadron X would number twenty-two crews, which Gibson would have to weld into a cohesive unit capable of carrying out a special low-level operation at night with a strange weapon in a maximum of eight weeks, later reduced to seven. His achievement in doing so must not be overlooked in the story of the operation itself – a 'terrific' feat, his adjutant concluded.

Nor should the important contribution of the groundcrew be ignored: the riggers, fitters, signallers, radar mechanics, administrative and non-specialist personnel. 'My first glimpse of Scampton,' recalls ACW Morfydd Gronland, among six WAAFs sent from RAF Waddington, 'filled me with the deepest gloom. It was a raw windy March day' and the WAAFs 'huddled up together in the back of an RAF van' that 'trundled into camp and lurched along uneven concrete roads' past the 'rain-swept runway'. They were then deposited at an ancient hut dubiously warmed by 'a pot-bellied stove'. Next morning they were warned that the Squadron Commander was 'a stickler for neatness' with a fetish about any slovenly appearance.

F/Sgt G. E. 'Chiefy' Powell, posted in from 57 Squadron, cast a wary eye over all the groundcrew newcomers, aware that other stations would have taken the opportunity to off-load 'scruffy buggers'. Several unwelcome guests were swiftly posted out, but not ACW Gronland, who was assigned to waitress duties in the Sergeants' Mess. There was a serious deficiency of all types of supplies. Powell had to scavenge for office equipment and mess furniture: 'Nobody knew where the chairs for the crew room came from, but I know,' he would later admit. Faced with a shortfall in sleeping accommodation, he quickly despatched a truck to commandeer surplus three-tier bunks from another station. On being shown his billet in a dilapidated wooden hut of First World War vintage destined to hold twenty-four men, and the cold-water ablutions close-by, Canadian radar specialist LAC H. K. 'Duke' Munro was distinctly unimpressed. His morale was not improved on learning that the accommodation had been officially condemned. Only sharp intervention from Gibson secured the necessary technical equipment from 5 Group stores, after an officious individual had quoted complicated regulations to deny Powell's requests. Clay, Munro's bomb-aimer, described how the aircrew 'did manage to put our flight offices into some sort of shape by putting up blackboards with rawlplugs and scraping old tables clean with bits of broken glass.' As one of Townsend's gunners, the breezy twenty-one year-old Londoner Doug Webb, observed, 'It was all fit and make fit.'

On 24 March 1943 Squadron X became officially operational, and three days later acquired a new identity: No. 617 Squadron.

Section I

Would We Get Them Again Now?

Selecting a New Crew

"When you think of the average age of the Squadron and you look at the people of twenty-one and twenty-two today, I'm not being derogatory about them, but would we get them again now, I wonder...?'
Harry Humphries, Adjutant, 617 Squadron

One of the things that struck Gary Johnstone, the film's director, and his team as they researched the story of that night in May 1943 was the sheer skill and daring of the crews who flew the missions. How on earth did they manage to fly over a blacked-out Europe at an average height of 100 feet all the way to Germany with only the moon for light? To try and better understand the skills of those original 617 crews, he had to devise a new way of telling their now so famous story. It was decided that a brand new Lancaster crew should be formed and trained to fly the same operation as the crew of AJ-N for Nan. This new crew would have to fly a simulator instead of a real Lancaster, but everything would be done to make their experience as close as possible to that of Les Knight and his crew. The question was, would it be possible to find the kind of crew that was needed?

Originally it was assumed that a group of qualified, experienced RAF pilots would fit the bill. To find them, and also to get an idea of 617 Squadron today, the team headed up to visit modern 617 Squadron based at Lossiemouth in the Scottish Highlands. Still a Bomber Squadron, all of 617 proudly wear the Dambusters badge, from aircrew to the civilian contractors who prepare their meals. The tools of the modern 617 Squadron are the jet engine and the computer. (Bombing has changed since 1943. The Geneva Convention of 1972 banned attacks on dams. And, surprising as it may seem, the modern Dambusters do not have a weapon that could do the job of an 'Upkeep' bouncing bomb.)

At 617 crews of two – pilot and navigator – fly the Panavia Tornado GR4, where technology now does many of the jobs once performed by a Lancaster crew of seven. Routes are planned on the Tornado Advanced Mission Planning Aid, or TAMPA. The navigator then takes all the computerised details of the operation on a Tornado Data Module or 'Brick' the size of a

The modern 617 Squadron practise low flying over Scotland using computer navigation systems.

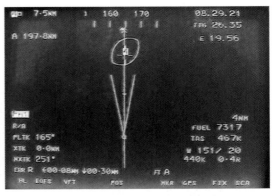

chocolate bar. This is plugged into the Tornado, whose Terrain Following Radar uses this information automatically to guide the aircraft to the target at supersonic speed 100 feet above the ground.

It was assumed that the hardest job in the new crew would be the pilot's. This was completely wrong. At Lossiemouth it was explained by an experienced navigator who had used maps and mental dead reckoning to calculate position and courses back in the pre-computer sixties and seventies that the type of navigation used in 1943 is a lost art that would have to be remastered. The title of Navigator in the RAF now has more to do with tradition than reality. In a Tornado the job is about managing weapon systems. Despite the generation gap between the Tornado and more advanced aircraft used by the Americans, the RAF has achieved an accuracy rate in its bombing of 98 per cent, nearly double the average of the United States Air Force and United States Navy. In Bomber Command in 1943, getting lost was one of the major factors behind casualty rates in more than ten per cent of operations. Fewer than five per cent of crews could actually find the targets they were going to bomb. It became clear to the film-makers on this trip that the navigator rather than the pilot would to be the crucial job.

College Hall at Cranwell.

And while the aircrews of modern 617 Squadron uphold the highest standards of their predecessors, it was soon realised on meeting with Squadron members that the hope of recruiting qualified flight crew there in Lossiemouth was starting to evaporate. Most of the skills the film-makers were looking for had all but vanished. Hope came from a casual remark made in the Officers' Mess.

Relaxing deep into an armchair, one of the pilots said that he'd forgotten most of the basic navigation he had learned several years ago. What was needed, he said, would be to get people who were still doing their basic flying training.

So it was back to basics – to the RAF College at Cranwell ('Cranditz' to officers and aircrew who train there). In College Hall the eyes of thousands of former inmates seem to follow you down the corridors from their photographs crammed on to the walls. Those in the earliest photographs, which date from the 1920s, wear uncomfortable-looking serge uniforms and puttees, which are swapped in later photographs for the familiar trousers and shoes; and after the Second World War women begin to appear. In one of the photographs Lucy Robinson, a newly commissioned officer, is seen receiving an award.

Squadron Leader Rob Wigham and Squadron Leader Dave Thomas assembled a group of willing candidates – thirty turned up in total, for the eight jobs that were on offer. Lucy, first glimpsed in the College Hall photographs, now a 25-year-old Flight Lieutenant, was the first in front of the audition committee. Lucy was waiting to start flying the VC10, and had previously been training to be a fighter pilot. She had experience on more aircraft types and flying techniques than anyone else interviewed.

Some of the candidates were distinctly nervous but all were fascinated by the experiment and enthralled by the stature of the Dambusters in RAF mythology, rivalled only by the Battle of Britain. Competition to be selected was keen, but now and then a candidate stood out.

Twenty-five-year-old Paul 'Branty' Brant was a trainee fighter pilot whose degree in Civil Engineering suggested a flair for the mental gymnastics required of a navigator. Andy Griffiths,

Lucy Robinson

Paul 'Branty' Brant

Andy Griffiths

Al Chevis

Stuart 'Molly' Molkenthin

Ben 'Tapper' Knight

Teri Livingstone

Frankie Buchler

twenty-six, who was soon to train to fly the Hercules transport aircraft, had an old friend who had been a Lancaster Wireless Operator. Al Chevis, aged twenty, who was soon to train as a Sergeant Air Electronics Operator in a Nimrod surveillance aircraft, had an uncle who had been a Lancaster Rear Gunner. Other Air Electronics Operators, whose job would soon be to operate radar and sonar equipment, were Stuart 'Molly' Molkenthin, twenty-six, and Ben 'Tapper' Knight, twenty-one. Teri Livingstone, who was older than the others at thirty-one, had had a previous career in the police, and was passionate about military history and her Ducatti 748 motorcycle. She seemed the most naturally suited for the experiment and was the only candidate chosen without further debate.

The last to be selected was twenty-five-year-old Frankie Buchler, who had just finished his training on the Shorts Turcano and would next be flying the Hawk in the last stage of his training as a fighter pilot.

Looking through the newly chosen crew, it was apparent immediately that their average age was identical to that of AJ-N: twenty-five years old. There were noticeable differences too. Although the officers in the new crew were still in training, they had all served longer in the RAF than anyone in AJ-N at the time of the Dams Raid. (The time taken to train on modern aircraft shows their complexity, and this training time is despite – or maybe because of – the modern technology that carries out much of the work once done by a Lancaster's crew.) Back in

Getting to grips with the history.

Above: Branty and Molly (left) and (right) Andy and Lucy discuss the achievements of 617 in 1943.

1943 there were no female aircrew, but this new crew contained two women. Another major difference was that none of the sergeants who were interviewed were pilots. In 1943 many of the pilots in 617 Squadron were non-commissioned officers – Les Knight himself had been a Sergeant Pilot until he was commissioned in December 1942 at the age of nineteen – but in the modern RAF all pilots are officers.

So for the next eight weeks, at a time they would otherwise have been waiting to start the next stage of their training, these eight aircrew would be taking part in an exciting and innovative piece of film-making. Their training for The *Dambusters* documentary would consist of historical research, training in navigation techniques used in 1943, and familiarising themselves with the Lancaster bomber by visiting and flying in surviving examples. Once they completed this specially devised training course they would all be told which of the various jobs on the crew they had been selected for. The final step would be intensive training on a massive purpose-built Simulator culminating in them actually flying the same mission in real time under the same conditions as their predecessors, Les Knight's AJ-N crew.

CHAPTER

5

Unique Weapon

Development of the 'Bouncing Bomb'

The day after he learned that the dams operation was to go ahead, on 27 February 1943, Wallis wrote, 'My fear now is that this important decision may have been arrived at too late.' Harris had been right to claim 'Upkeep' existed only 'within the imagination'. So far the largest version of it to be designed and tested had been roughly half-size – 4ft. 6in. in diameter.

That Saturday afternoon, Wallis began the first full-scale drawings of 'Upkeep'. Originally he had intended it as a near-spherical steel weapon, 7ft. 6in. in diameter, with its poles cut back effectively to make flat ends, which would allow attachment of the spinning mechanism. A cylindrical central core would hold the explosive charge inside an external steel casing. But Wallis had already discovered that the steel for this size of outer casing could not be guaranteed for two years, due to the pressure of other military requirements. Therefore he settled on a smaller charge cylinder, which could be cold-rolled and welded. The planned outer diameter of the sphere would be achieved by putting packing round the cylinder and binding 'great staves of wood' outside with six 1½-inch-diameter steel bands sunk in grooves. The result would resemble a large beer barrel.

Three hydrostatic pistols, standard Admiralty types for underwater detonation, and a self-destructive device would be inserted in the charge cylinder. The latter, fourth device would be fully armed once 'Upkeep' left an aircraft, in order to prevent the enemy from recovering Wallis's unique weapon if the hydrostatic pistols failed to function.

Although the drawings had still not been finalised, Wallis discussed sufficient details with RAF officers and civilian engineers on 2 March for manufacturing arrangements to be made. Vickers-Armstrongs agreed to produce the cylinders and wooden casings at its Elswick and Barrow works, then these would be sent to Royal Ordnance factories at Chorley and Woolwich for live and inert filling respectively. At Greenford, near

Manchester, A. V. Roe & Co. Ltd. (Avro) undertook to modify Lancasters (designated Type 464 Provisioning) destined for the Squadron and RAF Boscombe Down, where range and performance trials would be carried out. After listening to Wallis, Avro's chief designer, Roy Chadwick, suggested that the mid-upper turret of each Lancaster be removed to reduce drag. Wallis believed this a crucial innovation, which was in due

'Upkeep': Wallis originally intended a semi-circular shape with flattened ends. Note the outer wooden casing held in place by metal bands.

course approved by the Air Ministry; without it, the operation might never have been launched. The aircraft to be modified were Lancasters IIIs, powered by four Merlin 28 engines (built under licence by the Packard Motor Company of Detroit to American 'standards and measures').

On Thursday 4 March Wallis completed the design drawings of 'Upkeep', only to discover a major problem. V-shaped calliper arms, between which 'Upkeep' would be held before release, were to be fitted to the fuselage of each Lancaster at the sides of the bomb-bay. Such was the tightness of security that Wallis had never seen the specifications or design details of a Lancaster, so 'Upkeep' was too long; the design amendment to reduce the length was not apparently finished until 13 March. This delayed completion of its construction at the Vickers-Armstrongs works and inevitably slowed down the filling process. Wallis did not panic. 'My impression is that we shall come through all right as things are going far better than I thought would be possible.' And he received an encouraging letter from Sir Charles Craven, who had been so forthright on 23 February to Wallis's discomfort and dismay. 'I have seen the Chief of the Air Staff twice in the last week, and also Sir Wilfrid Freeman [his deputy]. They are taking intense interest in the whole scheme.'

By mid-March it had been decided to modify only twenty-three Lancasters, not thirty as first intended: twenty directly to 617 Squadron, and three for trial purposes. A charge of 6600lb of Torpex had now been agreed. Wallis was worried, however, that violent water disturbance created by one explosion would affect the accuracy of the following attacks. On 30 March an Admiralty scientist, Dr E. C. Bullard, allayed his fear by concluding that 'after five minutes, the height of the waves will be measured in inches rather than feet'. Not until 7 April, after exhaustive spinning tests in a rig on the ground, was Wallis satisfied that 'Upkeep' would not leap from the retaining callipers if rotated at more than 400r.p.m. to achieve the required back-spin.

To analyse the performance of the full-size weapon, more aerial trials were necessary. Because the level of the water at Chesil Beach (where the last test flights occurred on 8 and 9 March) was now too low, flying trials were transferred to a bombing range in the Thames estuary off the North Kent coast at Reculver, which could be easily cordoned off from unwelcome visitors. As each practice bomb was released from an aircraft a bulb flashed, and on the promenade A. D. Grant of Wallis's staff had four stop-watches to time the first three bounces, while another Vickers-Armstrongs employee, Herbert Jeffree, had equipment to determine their height and performance during the whole run. Nearby RAF Manston would act as the base for these critical trials. There the aircraft would be bombed up by Service personnel under the supervision of Vickers-Armstrongs' staff. Jeffree recorded that, when once required to insert a detonator into guncotton prior to loading an inert-filled practice weapon at Manston, nervous onlookers retreated a full 4 feet. That, he remarked, would have been a 'fat lot of good' if an explosion had occurred.

For the Reculver trials, one, then two, of the modified Lancasters would be added to the Wellington used at Chesil Beach. Vickers-Armstrongs' test pilots Summers and Handasyde would be joined by a seconded RAF officer, Sqn Ldr M. V. 'Shorty'

Opposite 'Upkeep' tests: Herbert Jeffree, one of Wallis's staff (left), supervises static dropping tests.

Reculver trials: the Lancaster, flying at right angles to the promenade (out of the pictures to the right) drops a practice 'Upkeep'. Note the final 'garden roller' shape.

Longbottom, and Avro's chief test pilot, Captain Sam Brown. At 0920 on Tuesday 13 April Wallis and Gibson were among the group of spectators who watched Handasyde in the Wellington fly east to west parallel to the shore towards two white marker buoys bobbing in the water, and drop an inert-filled 'Upkeep' from a height of 80 feet. The outer wooden cover burst on hitting the water, but the central steel cylinder ran on. Wallis thought the outcome 'excellent'.

Twice more that day, with one recording ciné camera mounted broadside to the flights on shore and another virtually ahead on a spit beneath the ruined towers of an old Norman church, Longbottom used the Lancaster for further drops. During the first flight, at 1108, he flew at 250 feet. Wallis waded out at low tide to retrieve fragments of the bomb, which had disintegrated, and reasoned that Longbottom had flown too high. As dusk fell, at 1907, the final flight that day was made at 50 feet. Amid the cascade of spray, the wooden casing again splintered (damaging the elevator of the Lancaster, which had difficulty in landing at Manston), but as with Handasyde earlier the steel cylinder bounced on. Wallis gave instructions to tighten the metal bars welded to the cylinder in preparation for the second series of Reculver trials. Just over a month before the raid, he still saw 'Upkeep' as a sphere.

Poor visibility caused postponement of the scheduled flights for Saturday 17 April, but did not prevent Wallis, to 'the delighted hoots' of onlookers, from plunging into the 'so inviting' sea for a nude bathe, afterwards drying himself 'with a pocket handkerchief'. Later that day, more conventionally, he and members of his staff rolled up their trousers to recover more pieces of the bombs shattered on 13 April. They soon gave up, the water being 'too deep and cold'.

On Sunday 18 April at 1100 Summers dropped the first of three spheres, all of which broke. But the cylinder of the one released at 1330 'held up' to bounce on for another 700 yards, the third time this had happened. Over a late sandwich lunch, in discussion with the scientist Professor G. I. Taylor, who had witnessed that morning's trials, Wallis took a momentous decision. He would dispense with the outer casing and internal packing. 'Upkeep' would become simply the central steel cylinder, the shape today recognised as 'the bouncing bomb'.

Three days later, on 21 April, Brown dropped two bare cylinders in succession. Both sank, and Wallis declared this trial 'a complete failure'. The attack on the dams lay little more than three weeks away, because the final date for its execution had now been advanced from 26 to 19 May. On 24 April Wallis met Gibson in his temporary office at Burhill Golf Club. Using diagrams of the Möhne, Wallis explained that the height of release (then set at 150 feet) and the speed of the attacking aircraft must be amended, otherwise the attack might well fail. He calculated that a height of 60 feet would be necessary, which in the face of flak would be extremely dangerous for the crews. Fortunately, Gibson agreed. This was another pivotal point, like the decision to abandon the wooden casing, in the last, critical stages of the development of 'Upkeep'. Moreover, there is some doubt as to whether a full-size cylinder had yet been dropped at Reculver.

For some unexplained reason, not all future test drops were made from 60 feet. Without doubt, though, at 0915 on 29 April Longbottom did release a full-size cylinder from 50 feet. It bounced for 670 yards, but deviated 30 feet off-track. At 1030 on Friday 30 April Longbottom dropped another bare 'Upkeep' from 65 feet in a flat calm. The bomb bounced four times, which Wallis announced 'a very good performance'. Two days later, on 2 May, Longbottom dropped a cylinder from 80 feet. Due to the rough sea this was less successful: three bounces and a 40-foot deviation left of track. Wallis was, however, now convinced that the operation could be flown, although Air Staff officers were more cautious. They wanted at least five more test drops from 60 feet at 210-220m.p.h. groundspeed with 'Upkeep' spinning at 500r.p.m. Wallis worked out that, if 'Upkeep' were dropped from 60 feet at 210m.p.h., the range from the distance achieved would be precisely 476 yards, half of which would be in the air before the first bounce. Just fourteen days remained before Operation Chastise.

The form of the trials at Reculver was altered during the first week of May. Canvas screens were erected on the promenade and the aircraft now flew towards them at right-angles to the shore. Cylinders falling short only disturbed the pebbles, while those that overshot ('long hops' to Handasyde) threatened to blow up mines sown in adjacent meadows to deter would-be invaders, or mutilate the farmer's grazing cows.

On 6 May, with Handasyde as observer, Longbottom flew at the new angle four times, though Wallis considered only one 'shot' satisfactory. After adjustment of the calliper arms at Manston, on 7 May 'Shorty did two good drops – direct hits'. Bad weather then intervened. Not until 11 May did Longbottom drop two 'Upkeeps' along the off-shore run, parallel to the beach. Both were spun at 500r.p.m. and released from 75 and 50 feet respectively. Neither deviated from track – the former bounced five times over 430 yards, the latter six times over 450 yards. The following day, Handasyde obtained similar results.

The most significant trial took place on 13 May, however. Flying south-west to north-east five miles off Broadstairs, Longbottom dropped a fully armed 'Upkeep' filled with Torpex explosive from 75 feet. It bounced seven times 'about 800 yards' without deviation before exploding. With Gibson beside him, Handasyde flew another Lancaster at 1000 feet and 1000 yards behind with a normal-speed camera on board to supplement the theodolite one positioned ashore on the North Foreland. The staff officer in Longbottom's rear turret noted that 'Upkeep' slowed to approximately 55m.p.h. after it hit the water, which meant that it could never endanger the crew if released properly. Films from the airborne and land-based cameras showed that the water spout rose to 1500 feet after 'Upkeep' detonated at an estimated 33 feet below the surface. 'Upkeep' was now officially 'sufficiently robust to withstand repeated impact with the water and soft targets and has satisfactory balance.'

One final test remained. Wallis was concerned that if 'Upkeep' hit the water too hard it might explode immediately. On Saturday 15 May, therefore, Handasyde once more flew off Broadstairs for a straight drop of 'Upkeep', without spinning, from 500 feet –

Live drop: 'Upkeep', filled with live explosive, is dropped off Broadstairs on 13 May. It bounced seven times and detonated exactly as planned. The last frame shows another Lancaster flying behind carrying Gibson to observe and two cameramen to film the drop.

although he later maintained it was more like 4000 feet. There was no explosion on the surface or below the water, for no hydrostatic pistol nor self-destructive device had been fitted. Not only were Wallis's residual doubts removed, but also the anxiety of those who feared that the relatively new explosive Torpex might be unstable if used in this way. A further, last unease was also erased: 'Upkeep' fell as soon as it was released by the bomb-aimer – there was no delay. Once it had shed its load, the Lancaster lifted suddenly and sharply to about 1000 feet, which would have the added advantage of confusing flak gunners when the aircraft were perilously exposed to dam defences.

The Duke of Wellington observed of the Battle of Waterloo: 'It was a damn'd close run thing.' That was true of 'Upkeep' development, too. The Dambusters Raid would be flown the very next day.

CHAPTER

6

Intense Training

Preparation for Attack

All the research, model experiments, flying trials and sheer hard work to perfect 'Upkeep' would be utterly pointless without the means of delivering it to the targets. Gibson was therefore equally under pressure to train his new squadron before 19 May, after which the level of water in the German reservoirs would become too low for a successful operation.

Soon after reaching Scampton on 21 March, Gibson settled on his two flight commanders. Apart from being experienced pilots, both were accomplished sportsmen: Sqn Ldr H. M. Young DFC, an Oxford rowing blue who had completed two bombing tours, and Sqn Ldr H. E. Maudslay, an accomplished middle-distance runner and former Captain of Boats at Eton. Their proven leadership qualities made them natural choices. Possessing considerable administrative ability (according to Plt Off Geoff Rice, 'He lived with a typewriter, a fantastic administrator') Young was an ideal deputy for Gibson in the coming weeks, when the Squadron Commander found himself called away to countless meetings and the Reculver trials. Young's addiction to yoga and snuff did not endear him to more ebullient spirits, but Leonard Cheshire bore witness to his unflappability. Once sheltering from a particularly unpleasant bombing raid, he produced a pack of cards and enquired 'Anyone for bridge?' Twice he had ditched while returning from an operation, acquiring thereby the nickname 'Dinghy'.

Sutherland, Knight's Canadian front gunner, who had known him in 50 Squadron, was among many aircrew at Scampton to express their admiration for Maudslay. 'He was a wonderful guy, a real gentleman.' He recalled that once a wireless operator, who had missed an operation through sickness, was devastated when his crew crashed. Realising the man's distress, Maudslay invited him to join his own crew. 'That's the kind of guy Maudslay was. A compassionate guy, who would take time to talk to an ordinary airman and was always friendly. I had the greatest respect for him.' Whittaker

(Martin's flight engineer) thought Maudslay 'quiet, kind, purposeful. Nothing was too much trouble.'

The day-to-day running of the squadron was in the capable hands of the adjutant, Flt Lt H. R. Humphries, whose appointment had not been planned. The officer allocated to the post wanted to live outside Scampton with his wife, but Gibson expected his adjutant to be on call twenty-four hours a day. Humphries was on the staff at Syerston, where Gibson had commanded 106 Squadron, and he whimsically ascribed his selection to the fact that he had made Gibson laugh when impersonating Winston Churchill in a station concert party. 'Gibson came round one night when I was messing around in one of the offices and said, "Would you like to join me as squadron adjutant?" I said, "Yes, please", and that's how it started.' Humphries would turn out to be an excellent choice. At Scampton he found that the adjutant was 'more or less personal assistant to the Squadron Commander'. He drafted squadron orders for him to sign, filtered requests for personal interviews and dealt with all correspondence, including that from higher authorities up to and including the Air Ministry, that was not reserved for the Squadron Commander's personal attention. The adjutant must leave his superior officer as much time as possible to concentrate on flying matters. Provision of squadron transport, rations and meals fell to him. The adjutant was 'a general dogsbody', dealing with everything from personal problems to leave applications and official car mileage allowance forms. His major responsibilities were the maintenance of squadron discipline and, when the squadron was operating, 'generally making sure the aircrew were well attended to'. In carrying out this wide range of duties on 617 Squadron, Humphries heavily relied on 'two blokes, they were my rock' – Powell and the orderly room sergeant, Jim Heveron – both of whose postings had been blocked by 57 Squadron's commander until 617 Squadron 'screamed'.

Gibson had met Wallis for the first time on 24 March in bizarre circumstances. He had travelled by rail and car, being picked up at Weybridge station by Summers, to see 'a scientist', and ended up in Wallis's office at Burhill. To the astonishment of both men, Gibson's name was not on the list of those cleared for a full briefing. Wallis, therefore, could show only some of the trial films, and give Gibson an overall summary of what had been going on and something of what was required. Thus far, he explained, only a half-size weapon had been tested. The eventual attack would, he believed, necessitate accurate release at 240m.p.h. at a height of 150 feet above smooth water after pulling out of a 2000-foot dive. Gibson had therefore left Burhill that evening with only a hazy, but daunting, impression of what lay ahead.

Three days later, on the day that Squadron X became 617 Squadron, the 5 Group SASO, Gp Capt H. V. Satterly, issued a 'most secret' order to Gibson, which revealed more details of the impending operation – though by no means all. 'No. 617 Squadron will be required to attack a number of lightly defended special targets.' Low-level navigation in moonlight would be needed over enemy territory 'with a final approach to the target at 100 feet and a precise speed, which will be about 240m.p.h.' Satterly anticipated aircraft to be despatched at 10-minute intervals to attack Target A. Once that had been destroyed, they would proceed to 'Target B, Target C and so on'. Giving no specific clue to the nature of those targets, Satterly continued that in preparation for a low-level attack 'it will be convenient to practise this over water', with crews able to release their 'mine' within 40 yards of a specific point. Satterly thus slightly expanded Wallis's recent briefing. The route to and from the target area must be planned to avoid flak, aerodromes and other defended localities. During daylight training, the pilot and bomb-aimer should wear dark glasses to simulate moonlight conditions, and a second pilot was to be carried in case of emergency. Satterly concluded by listing nine lakes suitable for practice, and that afternoon Flt Lt Bill Astell took off from Scampton to photograph them.

On 28 March, with Young and Hopgood on board, Gibson trailed a length of chain beneath his aircraft (possibly inspired by Finch Noyes's proposal in connection with his 1941 scheme) over Derwent Water near Sheffield to achieve the required height of 150 feet.

A later photograph of Group Captain H. V. Satterly, Senior Air Staff Officer of No 5 Group, who wrote the Dams Raid Operation Order and locked it each night in a safe during and after completion.

He almost consigned them all to a watery grave. It was clear that getting and keeping that height in a Lancaster at night would be tricky – and extremely dangerous.

Having survived this ordeal, the very next day, 29 March, Gibson was summoned to Grantham where Cochrane revealed the targets. Gibson admitted relief that his crews would not be sent to sink the powerful battleship *Tirpitz*, which was then lurking menacingly in a Norwegian fjord. RAF Medmenham had built a model of the Möhne Dam and reservoir for briefing purposes, and before the operation would also make one for the Sorpe. All the other target dams, including the Eder, would have only written and photographic information for the crews to study, as Gibson did on 29 March. However, Gibson could now travel south for a more comprehensive meeting with Wallis. Summers, who was present, pointed out that the explosion would occur in the water well behind the delivering aircraft, so the parapet of the dam wall would protect it – an optimistic forecast that could not be challenged. Gibson did, however, firmly reject Wallis's proposal that to guarantee accuracy the operation should take place in daylight. That would be suicidal.

By 24 April all surplus aircrew manpower had been shed, and the number of crews reduced to twenty-one. Sgt Lovell's crew had returned to 57 Squadron and had been replaced by that of Sgt Divall. F/Sgt Lanchester and his crew had opted to leave the Squadron, because Gibson wanted to replace the navigator. The Squadron Commander was, in Shannon's term, 'a martinet' pursuing high standards. With the task ahead, he had to be.

Throughout April Gibson reported that 'daily intensive flying training (was) carried out, when weather permitted' – along selected cross-country routes, none of them of less than three hours duration. This was not universally appreciated by the civil population. Stories circulated about clergymen being blown off their bicycles into sodden ditches, panic-stricken labourers diving from the top of haystacks and cattle stampeding. Not all were lurid inventions. Maudslay returned from one foray with foliage protruding from the Lancaster's undercarriage, and people close to Lake Bala in Wales officially complained at the low-flying antics. Farmers even blamed 617 Squadron for fluctuation in their cows' milk yield.

Doc Sutherland described this phase of training: 'I guess we had a lot of cross-country up as far as Scotland and round the Lake District, just low-level. I remember those canals in northern England or Scotland and flying along those, and I think it was all navigation and map reading. It had to be, we were training, Johnny was the expert map reader and Hobday of course was a marvellous navigator and together they just made a real team.' Grayston, the flight engineer, remembered going under power cables during training near East Lynn, and on one occasion flying down a canal that ran into the sea. This led the Lancaster at low level into the midst of 'a whole load of ships and yachts whose sails were violently disturbed by the down draught'. For that they 'got into a lot of trouble'.

George Johnson (McCarthy's bomb-aimer) had more specific memories. On one of the cross-country runs they had to cross tulip fields near Spalding. 'It was a bit pathetic to see those poor old tulips just being flagged down by the slip stream', and he wondered what compensation the farmers received. Like Grayston, he recalled flying

Low-level practice: a 'borrowed' Lancaster being flown soon after the formation of 617 Squadron.

under rather than over 'some electric cables across a canal at Sutton Bridge' via which 'many of the cross-countries came back'. McCarthy's crew did not use the Derwent Dam in training, but they often flew along canals with the wing tips either inside or just above the banks. Rivers were found to be too dangerous, due to their many bends. Humphries asked Knight if he could fly with him on one practice, not 'knowing we were going to fly at low level...We took off and next thing I knew we were flying across fields and cows were running up walls and the horses were galloping all over the place, and we were sort of just going over the top of electricity pylons. I felt the use for the toilet at that time. It was very exhilarating but it was very frightening.' 'I didn't volunteer to go up again,' Humphries added.

Because the crews flew as and when aircraft became available, meals had to be ready almost continuously. In the Sergeants' Mess, Morfydd Gronland described a typical scene after a training flight. 'The doors would burst open and the aircrew would swarm in shouting boisterously. We young WAAFs had to endure a barrage of good-humoured banter: "How's your sex life?" ... "I dreamed about you last night" ... "Please serve us in the nude". Then someone would ask, "What's the collective noun for WAAFs?" And a chorus would answer "A mattress."' But ACW Gronland recalled: 'We took it all in good part because we knew the great strain they were under and the dangers they would soon face.'

As the month closed, Gibson could report that all crews were competent to navigate by night from and to pinpoint locations at low level. Exercises with standard 11½lb practice bombs had been conducted at the Wainfleet range on the Wash. There 'two white cricket boards' (30 feet by 20 feet) had been erected 700 feet apart to represent the towers on top of the Möhne Dam. With a special 'range-finder sight' these were used to determine the point of release. Since 26 April crews had been instructed to bomb from the lower height of 60 feet at 210m.p.h. In the last week of April thirty-one exercises were carried out at Wainfleet, with 284 bombs dropped with an average error of 39 yards. Air-to-air gunnery practice with towed targets and air-to-sea practice with floats had also taken place. Sutherland explained that sometimes they 'dropped a smoke bomb out in the Wash and would then go and shoot off the starboard or port side to get the deflection right' before 'shooting that smoke bomb up pretty good.' In making his report to the Station Commander, Whitworth, Gibson noted that flying training would now make concentrated use of the Eyebrook Reservoir, two miles south of Uppingham in Rutland.

This reservoir, with a straight dam wall and usually full in May, supplied water for the Stewart & Lloyd steelworks at Corby. Years later, Cochrane explained that to secure its use he took the works manager 'out for a slap-up lunch'. The manager, Mr G. C. S. Oliver, strenuously denied having benefited from this example of 'bribery and corruption'. Records simply show that on 3 May Mr G. Le Mare, director of the Corby (Northants) & District Water Company, met RAF representatives, who 'explained that they wanted a sheet of water for special and urgent tests of some new device during the next three weeks.' Having been assured that nothing would be dropped or fired and that no damage would be done, Le Mare agreed. The following day 'four special canvas targets' were placed 'on top of the dams on poles fixed in barrels of concrete'. The four 'targets' were grouped in twos to simulate the towers on the Möhne Dam.

Although the Squadron had already intermittently flown over the reservoir in training before the appearance of the mock towers, specific exercises began at 1600 on 4 May. The next day Oliver wrote: 'Lancaster bombers have been flying low over the reservoir last night and today. They fly between two targets which are put on the dam … and are in no way doing any harm.' Nearby residents were not so relaxed. At first they leapt from their beds and dashed to the air-raid shelters, fearing an enemy bombing raid. As they got used to the repeated flights, with aircraft firing 'purple flares' as they pulled up over the dam, many gathered to watch. Others, though, bombarded the letter pages of the press with complaints about the 'frightening' roar, that 'the house shook' or a terrified wife had dived under the bed. Three miles south of Colchester, Abberton Reservoir – without dummy towers – served a similar purpose for the Eder Dam. There, however, inhabitants were not close, and curious onlookers were kept at a safe distance. They could only see the Lancasters fire a flare as they crossed the dam before pulling up steeply. There was an unpleasant side effect to these manoeuvres and the continuous low-level flying – air sickness – for which the Squadron medical officer, Fg Off M. W. Arthurton, provided 'appropriate medicine'.

The high standard of training – and eventually the effectiveness of Operation Chastise – could not have been attained without four crucial innovations. The use of dark glasses to create artificial darkness had only limited success, so an American development, Synthetic Night Flying Equipment, was acquired. It entailed fitting blue celluloid to the cockpit windows and the front and rear gunners' positions, with amber-tinted goggles for crew members to wear. However, when the goggles were removed outside the aircraft everything around appeared red, and aircrew quickly learned to don dark glasses until their vision had re-adjusted. (Even so, F/Sgt Len Sumpter – Shannon's bomb-aimer – believed that a subsequent deterioration in his eyesight stemmed from this activity.) The first Lancaster fitted with the American equipment at the Scampton workshops became available on 11 April, but only one more, instead of the hoped-for total of six, was modified in this way. None the less, the two Lancasters were 'very efficient', according to Gibson, and were used 'extensively'.

The second special aid concerned the point at which 'Upkeep' must be released over the reservoir. Study of published technical data and reconnaissance photos showed that the two towers on top of the Möhne Dam, which covered access to machinery operating the sluices, were approximately 700 feet apart, hence the position of the 'sight boards' at Wainfleet and the screens at the Eyebrook. Wg Cdr C. L. Dann, supervisor of aeronautics at the Boscombe Down Experimental Centre, used this information to construct a simple triangular wooden sight, with a peephole at its apex and two nails at the extremities of its base. Each bomb-aimer would hold a piece of wood fitted below the peephole, which he squinted through. As an aircraft approached a target, the distant dams visually came outwards. When the nails and the Wainfleet screens, Eyebrook 'canvas targets' or the actual towers during the operation coincided, the bomb-aimer would press the release mechanism. After another trial flight over the Derwent Reservoir, making use of the two towers on its dam, Gibson expressed his satisfaction with the device. Mathematical calculations were then made to work out the figures appropriate to the different target dams.

Gibson had already demonstrated almost fatally the difficulty of judging the very low height at which 'Upkeep' must be dropped. This problem was referred to the MAP, where it landed on the desk of the civilian DSR and Cambridge-educated scientist, Benjamin Lockspeiser. He recalled that in 1942 Coastal Command had briefly and unsuccessfully used two spotlights fitted under the wings of its Hudson patrol aircraft to assist in the detection and attacking of U-boats caught on the surface. Having read the papers – 'a confirmation of the need to write up even failed experiments' – Lockspeiser concluded that the double beams had failed due to choppy water, which would not be evident in reservoirs. Later he regretted that, unlike the seductive myth, no scantily clad chorus girls in an orchestrated 'leg show' assisted him in this quest. When he was approached by the makers of the 1955 film, Lockspeiser described this part of the plot as ludicrous, but agreed to the discovery being falsely attributed to Gibson, whom he considered 'a very brave man'.

In April 1943 Lockspeiser went to Grantham and persuaded Cochrane that this method might work for Operation Chastise. Carrying out ground tests at the Royal Aircraft Establishment (RAE) Farnborough, however, Lockspeiser realised that the structure of the Lancaster made the Hudson alignment impossible. Arguing that cameras would be useless at the intended low level, he reasoned that one Aldis lamp should be placed in the normal front camera position near the bomb-aimer's compartment in the nose, and the second at the rear of the bomb-bay, where it would not be obscured because the bomb-bay doors would be removed for this operation. An alternative rear position further aft, where the downward-firing ventral gun had been removed for the Dams Raid, was briefly considered but discarded. The positions therefore chosen for the two Aldis lamps were 20 feet apart – the front to the port of centre, the rear in the centre of the fuselage, respectively angled 30 degrees and 40 degrees to starboard, with the rear lamp slanted forward. The beams then formed a figure of eight when the aircraft was flying at the designated height. To achieve the necessary accuracy the navigator stood behind the flight engineer on the pilot's right and looked out of the Perspex blister aiming to get the circles touching just forward of the leading edge of the starboard wing. The navigator's job at this point in the operation was to advise the pilot whether to fly higher or lower before settling on the correct height.

Maudslay flew a Lancaster to Farnborough for the lamps to be fitted, and at Scampton demonstrated them before a sceptical audience. Gibson liked what he saw. The Spotlight Altimeter Calibrator (its official name) had been accepted, and the other 617 Squadron aircraft were duly modified. Crews then practised over Scampton's runways, where Plt Off Ivan Whittaker, Martin's flight engineer, spent many hours in darkness cross-checking their height with a theodolite. He also supervised another exercise in which crews dived towards a white line painted on the turf, flew level, then climbed when they reached a second line; the lines were soon replaced with tarpaulins, which were larger and easier to identify from altitude.

Using the Aldis lamps, the crews moved on to flying over the Wash, the North Sea and convenient canals. Gibson became concerned that these illuminations would become a magnet to enemy gunners in action and, moreover, 'a glassy calm' – the conditions anticipated – had not been experienced. Not until 10 May (a mere nine days before the cut-off date) were Gibson's worries about the lamps eased. Re-adjustment to cope with a height of 60 feet rather than 150 feet had been satisfactorily made and a way found of stopping the rear lamp from being covered in oil.

The fourth, and in reality the most important, innovation was the modified Type 464 Provisioning Lancaster. The first reached the Squadron on 8 April, then twelve more by the end of that month. This allowed the ten 'borrowed' aircraft, on which the crews had been practising, to go back to their own squadrons. Eyeing the strange machines without bomb-bay doors or mid-upper turrets, squadron wags dubbed them 'abortions' and the two 'cymbal-like contraptions' dangling underneath as 'clappers'. Humphries, the adjutant, was surprised when 'instead of having a bomb-bay, these aircraft turned up with long legs on them.' All the modified Lancasters were in the ED series with the suffix 'G' (Guard) added to their individual numbers. Once at Scampton, more minor alterations were carried out under the direction of the engineering officer, Flt Lt C. C. 'Capable' Caple.

A Type 464 Provisioning Lancaster: note the absence of the mid-upper turret and bomb-bay doors. The single ventral gun, aft of the RAF roundel, was also removed for the Dams Raid.

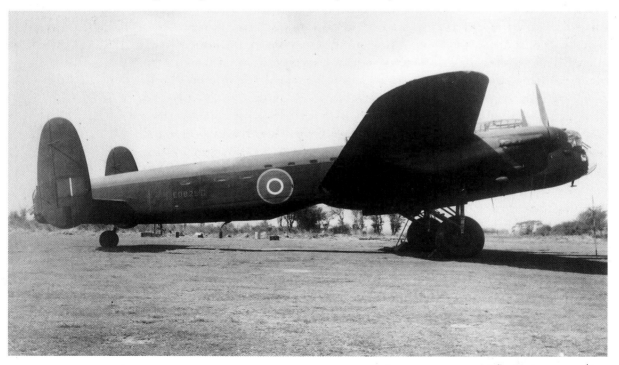

The strain on the groundcrew was intense during the training period. Normally, when a station knew that it would not be flying an operation that night, there was less of a sense of urgency about the daily maintenance tasks. At Scampton, in the workshops and on the exposed hard stands where the Lancasters were parked, activity could be seen all day and every day, with full advantage taken of Double British Summer Time (making sunset well after 2100). Before they left the station, the ten 'borrowed' Lancasters were flown so frequently that structural fatigue seemed likely. After one exercise, maintenance personnel discovered that the sturdy IFF (Identification Friend or Foe) equipment had been severely damaged by a practice bomb bouncing upwards when released at low level. On another occasion Gibson and the Rice inspected a Lancaster on which four of the bolts that held the panels to the centre section of the fuselage had been sheered, due to the constant buffeting at low level. This, like other machines with similar damage, had to be patched up quickly.

During these weeks, the crews not only learned to cope with the extra unusual demands of the forthcoming operation, but in some cases were also getting to know their new colleagues. As Dave Rodger, McCarthy's rear gunner, pointed out, every time they flew on operations 'it was seven men against the Reich'. Later reports held that the smaller of the two gunners was deployed in the front turret, but most crews put their more experienced in the rear whatever his size.

Crews tended to be self-sufficient, as experience with the Dann sight illustrated. Many soon realised that at low level the aircraft tended to bounce around, making it difficult for the bomb-aimer to hold the contraption firmly in one hand, the other

Bombing up: note 'Upkeep' loaded on the rear Lancaster, while the calliper arms and belt for rotating 'Upkeep' are visible on the nearer aircraft.

71

being needed to activate the bomb-release mechanism. In Shannon's crew the navigator, Fg Off D. R. Walker DFC RCAF, and the bomb-aimer, Len Sumpter, worked out an alternative system. Instead of Dann's sight, they drew two blue chinagraph marks on the clear vision panel in front of Sumpter. The bomb-aimer could then lie prone supported by his forearms, using the marks in place of the nails to focus on the towers, with string attached to the screws on each side of the panel drawn back taut to the bridge of his nose to fulfil the function of Dann's peephole. In Knight's crew Hobday, the navigator, and Johnson, the bomb-aimer, devised a similar system based upon the largest possible triangle involving the practice sight screen, marks on the clear vision panel, and Johnson's eye. Like Sumpter, Johnson used string attached to the retaining screws of the clear vision panel with an additional refinement: double marks on the panel to take into account the width of the practice screens (and ultimately, the dam towers). In Munro's crew, the bomb-aimer, Sgt J. H. Clay, effectively used the screws on the clear vision panel instead of Dann's nails or marks on the panel. In consultation with his navigator, Fg Off F. G. Rumbles, he attached string of a predetermined length and drew it back to his right eye. Some bomb-aimers, however, did retain the Dann sight.

Aircrew still had no inkling of the true nature of their target. Sgt Dudley Heal, Brown's navigator, recalled that the favourite guess was *Tirpitz*, though Martin's rear gunner, the Australian F/Sgt T. D. 'Tammy' Simpson, thought it 'something to do with U-boats', as did many in Knight's crew. Gibson was at pains to maintain their ignorance and was ruthless in enforcing security, rightly as Whittaker afterwards emphasised. Simpson wrote in his diary: 'Bags of security gen and various threats to those who were found from now on speaking or writing about the job.' The Squadron Commander, therefore, reacted swiftly and angrily by complaining to Cochrane that 617 Squadron's armament officer, Plt Off H. Watson, had been shown 'sectional drawings of certain objectives, a map of the Ruhr showing these objectives [and] various sketches in connection with "Upkeep"', while attending a course off-station early in May. Even Gibson himself did not then have this detailed information, and 'no other member of the squadron had been told, nor will they know until they are briefed for the operation'. What had happened was 'criminal': 'a most secret file' had been shown to a junior officer. Cochrane backed Gibson, the complaint found it way to Bomber Command headquarters at High Wycombe, and 5 Group commander was assured that appropriate disciplinary action had been taken. Closer to home, Gibson publicly condemned an aircrew member for indiscreet use of the telephone. When a senior intelligence officer returned from a visit to the Air Ministry indicating that he knew the targets, he became distinctly reticent after a visit to Gibson's office. Post-war, the Australian navigator Lance Howard praised Gibson's 'outstanding influence' on the squadron. 'Though we did not see a great deal of him, he seemed to set a standard of perfection in all our training and the final preparation. It's called leadership – how do you define it?' While acknowledging that he was 'very strict, a disciplinarian', Doc Sutherland suspected that he had 'some kind of hang-up' with the Canadians, possibly because they were 'too brash'. To his adjutant, Gibson had 'tremendous self- belief'. 'I don't think anybody could fault Gibson from the point of view of being commanding officer. When you went into his office, by his presence you knew he was the boss, and I suppose that's how it's got to be really… He wasn't too familiar with people, he kept them at a distance. We went out together occasionally for a beer and he was always "Sir".' Gibson 'wasn't a sentimental bloke. He could be a bit caustic. But he was a leader.'

That leadership included recognition of genuine medical problems. Fg Off J. Wickens (his rear gunner on 106 Squadron) recalled that he was at pains not to have anybody branded with 'Lack of Moral Fibre'. Arthurton, the 617 Squadron medical officer, confirmed that when he approached Gibson on behalf of an aircrew member 'obviously unable to contemplate the strain of this particular type of work' during training, Gibson readily agreed to his being posted out as unfit for duty due to illness.

The pace of the training and preparation quickened at the beginning of May. Gibson reported that between 30 April and 6 May, thirty-one exercises involving 168 bombing attacks at Wainfleet had taken place. Practice 'Upkeeps' had been prepared and balanced so that 'on or about 10, 12 or 13 May' crews could drop them at Reculver – the first time that they would see Wallis's weapon. From 1200 on Friday 7 May squadron leave would be stopped.

The previous day, 6 May, Gibson called together all pilots and the squadron's armament and engineering officers, Watson and Caple. Agreeing that achieving the required navigational accuracy had been 'absolute hell', he laid down arrangements for an important night exercise. Three formations, each of three aircraft, would fly the special route to the Eyebrook and Abberton reservoirs in turn, attacking at exactly 60 feet as directed by Gibson via radio-telephony (R/T) at those dams. He did not reveal that this represented the plan for the Möhne and Eder dams. Six other crews would do a practice attack on the Derwent Dam, flying south over the Howden and Derwent reservoirs to simulate the attack at right-angles then still intended at the Sorpe Dam. The remaining aircraft, destined to be the Mobile Reserve for the operation, would practise bombing aided by the Aldis lamps at Wainfleet. Caple must have 'maximum serviceability' of all aircraft round the clock from now on, and Watson the 'Upkeeps' filled with live explosive balanced and ready by 12 May. Young was to ensure that the all-up weight of the Lancasters did not exceed 63,000lb. Stirrups were to be provided for all front gunners to keep their feet out of the bomb-aimer's hair, and a second altimeter fitted to the windscreen to prevent the pilot having to look down at a vital moment.

That night, 6/7 May, the eighteen available Type 464 Provisioning Lancasters flew the planned night exercise, and a major communications deficiency that had already been noted in training was confirmed. The air-to-air reception of the TR1196 R/T set, so critical for Gibson to co-ordinate the attacks at the dams, proved unsatisfactory. Very High Frequency (VHF) Type 1143 sets used in fighters were rapidly installed in time for Maudslay and Young to test them on the evening of 9 May. Meanwhile, Flt Lt

Off-duty: Gibson in relaxed mood. David Shannon, who flew with Gibson on 106 and 617 Squadrons, said that off-duty he was 'one of the boys'.

R. E. G. Hutchison had organised booths in the crew rooms for wireless operators to practise R/T procedures.

During the second week of May, Watson and the armourers worked incessantly to get 'Upkeep' ready. As each arrived from the filling factory, machine work had to be carried out to achieve the correct balance. The 'Upkeeps' were hung in turn under one of the modified Lancasters for centrifugal balancing between the two calliper arms. A sheet of steel plate with two holes drilled in it was bolted to one side. If it proved too heavy it was removed and returned to the machine shop. There LAC Arthur Drury took metal off the plate to reduce the weight and the process was repeated as often as necessary until the correct balance was achieved.

On 10 May Satterly sent the only copy of the draft Operation Order to Scampton, 'written as you can see by my own fair hand', asking Whitworth and Gibson to study it. As a result some amendments were made. At this stage, with the attack ominously close, no live 'Upkeep' had yet been dropped, nor had any 617 Squadron pilot even flown with the practice version. On 11 May, however, Gibson and two other pilots flew at right angles to the promenade at Reculver to attack the mock towers. In his log book the Squadron Commander wrote: 'Low level. Upkeep dropped at 60 feet. Good run of 600 yards.' Not all crews went to Reculver then or later, among them McCarthy's, so several neither dropped nor saw 'Upkeep' in practice.

The following day more 617 crews bombed at Reculver, but Munro damaged the tailplane of his aircraft after releasing 'Upkeep' from too low a height. That Lancaster could be repaired, as could others that suffered similarly, as Knight's flight engineer explained. The Aldis lamps were not used at Reculver, and 'we were told to drop as low as possible, but we had no idea what our height was. The instruments, working on atmospheric pressure, weren't accurate enough. We dropped ours and the water splash from the mine [a practice, inert-filled 'Upkeep'] badly damaged our machine. The tailplane and the back end was like a sardine can where the water had hit it.' Maudslay experienced the same problem on 13 May, but his aircraft was so 'badly damaged' that it could not be repaired. This left only nineteen aircraft for twenty-one crews. For the fourth day running, on 14 May, 617 Squadron crews practised at Reculver, where Wallis recorded his appreciation of their ability to 'place' the weapon 'on the beach with remarkable accuracy'. He was now satisfied that they would be able to release 'Upkeep' in accordance with the tight limits required. Knight's front gunner Sutherland explained that crew's experience at Reculver. 'We were all a little apprehensive about dropping this spinning thing, which vibrated the whole aircraft. I think we got three bounces and then it rolled up on the beach.' But 'then we were more curious about what we were going to do with this thing. We really couldn't figure it out.'

During the night of 14-15 May the nineteen available Type 464 Provisioning Lancasters flew their last practice exercise before Operation Chastise. Gibson wrote in his log book: 'Full dress rehearsal on Uppingham Lake and Colchester Reservoir. Completely successful.' Fewer than forty-eight hours remained before the real thing.

Section II

Working Together
Training the New Crew

'... successful navigation can only be achieved when there is complete co-operation between the navigator and other members of the crew ...'
'Air Navigation', Air Council Publication, 1941

As they started their training for the Dambusters raid, the modern RAF crew were certain of one thing: no one wanted to be the navigator.

Navigation training for the new crew was devised by Sqn. Ldrs. Rob Wigham and Dave Thomas, both experienced pilots with the RAF. As flying instructors both know navigation inside out, but they still found it astonishing that the crew of AJ-N had flown across a blacked-out wartime Europe for hours on end at a height rarely exceeding 100 feet. However, the Operation Order issued to 617 Squadron in 1943 stressed the low-level aspect of Operation Chastise, as did the Navigation Log kept by the navigator of AJ-N for Nan, Sydney Hobday. Unfortunately 'Hobby' died in March 2000, but his detailed and accurate log is a perfect record of the route actually taken by his aircraft – and the height it was flown at – an average of 100 feet. Undeniable proof.

All of this served to unsettle the crew, as did the 1941 RAF *Air Navigation manual*, which brought home to them the fact that they would have to learn fast to use their brains rather than a computer.

The new crew practising their navigational skills.

Air Navigation is the art of guiding an aircraft from one place to another, and of fixing its position when required. The Air Navigator is assisted in his task by instruments that indicate the height and speed and direction of the aircraft through the air; while other instruments enable him to make observations of terrestrial objects and celestial bodies. Aided by these observations the progress and position of the aircraft relative to the ground may be deduced by the process of Dead Reckoning.

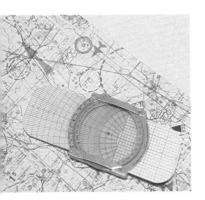

The modern version of the 1943 Navigation Computer.

The new crew were given the same scale maps as the Dambusters – 1:250,000 – a scale now used only by RAF helicopters, so none of the new crew were familiar with them. They were also given a rare original Navigation Computer – a combination circular slide rule and velocity plotter – similar to that used by navigators on the Dams Raid. It was expected that this would confound them, but it turned out that the design was so good that it is still used by the RAF (albeit now made of plastic instead of bakelite and steel).

The fact is that navigation techniques have not changed at all since 1943, only the technology of calculation, and this became clear as the new crew watched the 1943 training film *Nought Feet*. It stressed the importance of having clear landmarks to follow that can be easily identified at low level. With no modern-day computers to help them, every part of a route had to be carefully planned and positions constantly calculated using time, speed and direction. Even modern jet pilots wrestle with it, and their aircraft are so fast that the effect of wind is negligible. In the Lancaster windspeed had a crucial effect and if neglected

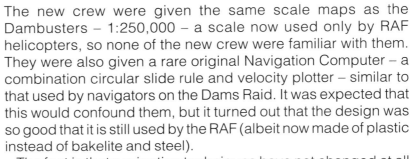
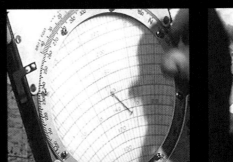
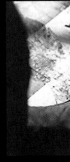

NOUGHT FEET

A FILM ON LOW FLYING NAVIGATION TECHNIQUE

would result in disaster. The more the new crew learned, the more they realised that their eight weeks was not going to be a holiday – it was going to be very hard work indeed. This insight really increased the awe and respect they felt for the crew of 1943.

The morning after the Annual Dinner the new crew turned up at 617 Squadron's old base at Scampton looking a little the worse for wear – as did Scampton. Today only a small part of the base is used, and standing in Guy Gibson's old office the crew felt disappointed at the smell of damp and the moss thriving on the inside window sill. The old grass runway had been replaced by a concrete one long ago, but in fact the hangars on the flight line, cleared of modern cars for the day's filming, looked just like they did in 1943. So immersed were the crew in 617 history that gazing out of the window it wasn't a huge leap to imagine a line of loaded Lancasters waddling out to the runway from Dispersal.

It was time to meet a Lancaster Bomber in the flesh – not far from Scampton, at the former RAF bomber base that is now the Lincolnshire Aviation Heritage Centre in East Kirkby. This was be the first time the crew had been on board the famous machine of the Dambusters raids. They were joined for the day by three Lancaster veterans – a Wireless Operator, Navigator and Pilot – to share their memories and to advise them on the jobs they would soon have to do.

The Lancaster interior is a narrow obstacle course filled with protrusions and obstructions on which to bang heads and scratch arms. Yet former Wireless Operator Larry Curtis moved through the fuselage with an ease and grace instilled over many flights and uncannily not forgotten after sixty years. The Wireless Operator's position is enclosed and you can't see outside very easily, but Larry liked it that way. He preferred not to look outside

A sequence from *Nought Feet*, the instructional film used by the RAF in the 1940s to train crew on the skills required for successful low-flying.

Above The team meeting veterans from the mission.

Right The veterans against a familiar background: (left to right) Ray Graystone, Larry Curtis and Alex McKie.

and see the explosions that threatened to destroy him. Next door is the navigator's work table. Another 617 Squadron veteran, Alex McKie, gave tips on how to deal with the problems of wind and navigating at low level.

Surprisingly the third veteran was a woman, Lettice Curtis. Although it would be years before the RAF had female aircrew, Lettice flew Lancasters as a pilot with the Air Transport Auxiliary, a ferry organisation that delivered planes to the bases as needed, releasing much-needed RAF pilots for operational flying. In 1943 George Chalmers, Wireless Operator of AJ-O for Orange, had been amazed to see Lettice deliver a modified Dambusters Lancaster to Scampton. Lettice spent an hour talking to Lucy in the East Kirkby Lancaster. Everyone present was struck by the how she and Lucy seemed like the same woman sixty years apart.

The simulated mission would be flown in the crew's comfortable Nomex flying suits, but while at East Kirkby they tried negotiating the various crew positions dressed in the same flying gear worn sixty years ago. Most Bomber Command operations were flown at over 20,000 feet, needing very warm clothing; the standard flying uniform was 'Suits, Aircrew', a serge wool blouse and trousers popular for their comfort at the time. For our modern crew it was the most uncomfortable thing they had ever worn. On top of this came a rubberised 1941-

Lettice Curtis meets Lucy.

pattern life-jacket, Observer's parachute harness and a leather flying helmet, which must be strapped painfully tightly on to the head to be able to hear with the primitive earphones. There is also an oxygen mask, of which Guy Gibson had bad memories: '...they are worn continuously ... because the pilot has no time to take his hand off the wheel and put the microphone up to his face. The result is that one gets quite chapped after six hours with the thing on.'

The crew felt that they learned a lot from the astonishingly crisp memories of the octogenarian veterans.

After initial research and training, the RAF instructors were finally able to make their recommendations as to which crew should be matched to which position in the newly constructed Lancaster Simulator. Rear Gunner, Front Gunner, Radio Operator, Engineer, Bomb Aimer, Pilot and Navigator were the positions up for grabs. The RAF instructors recommended that

The team getting to grips with the Lancaster and the roles they would play on their mission.

Branty took on the dreaded Navigator's job, and he was delighted by the challenge. The rest of the positions were handed out. The Bomb Aimer, who would have his finger on the trigger and also the vantage point in the nose, would be Molly. Andy and Al would be the Wireless Operator and Rear Gunner, Teri the Front Gunner. The mission would be flown and captained by Lucy, assisted by Tapper as Flight Engineer.

As Navigator, Branty would be blind to the outside world – deep in the belly of the plane, maps spread out on his table with only a tiny angle-poise lamp for light – and would depend on Molly to map-read and be his eyes. Lucy would need Branty to tell her where to fly and Tapper to help her control the aircraft. Teamwork would be absolutely vital – the mission would fail if they didn't all come together. Without radio operator Andy the crew would have no links with the other aircraft and would be unable to receive information from England. And without the two Gunners, Teri and Al, to protect them, the crew would be sitting ducks.

The last part of the crew's training at Cranwell was a sortie in a Jetstream multi-engined trainer flown by Lucy and navigated by Branty using Molly's eyes. The target was a windmill in the Yorkshire Dales. Lucy flew the Jetstream out of Cranwell at 2000 feet before descending to 200 feet for most of the flight. All went well. If anything, Branty was a little bored. The fighter jock started to think that his new role wouldn't be that challenging after all. But this would all soon change. In the Simulator the crew would face a vertical learning curve, training for a mission that they were only just now starting to understand.

Mounting Tension

48 Hours to Take-Off

Those last forty-eight hours were packed with activity. At 0900 on Saturday 15 May the Air Ministry sent an 'immediate most secret message' to Bomber Command at High Wycombe: 'Op. CHASTISE. Execute at first suitable opportunity.' In turn, Bomber Command alerted 5 Group headquarters at Grantham. During the morning Satterly finalised the Operation Order that contained one important change to his draft of five days earlier. This had included the seven target dams proposed by Wallis in his paper 'Air Attack on Dams'. Now the Henne was omitted, almost certainly because of a flak concentration around the small port of Meschede close by. That left six dams for attack.

Four were connected with the Ruhr. The Möhne Dam lay seven miles south of Soest and twenty-six miles east of Dortmund, at the junction of the Möhne and Heve rivers flowing northwards into the Ruhr River. Holding back 134 million cubic metres of water, the gravity dam, 650 metres (2133 feet) long, curved into the reservoir. It tapered upwards from the base, measuring 34.02 metres (112 feet) wide at the bottom, and 6.25 metres (21 feet) at the top, along which a roadway ran. Astride the structure, spanning the road and covering access to the machinery and inspection galleries below, 196 metres (639 feet) apart, were the two towers that would aid the bomb-aimers. From the centre of the dam, looking up the reservoir, a wooded spit of land topped by the Hevers Berg (262 metres – 557 feet – high) divided the two rivers before they merged in front of the dam. The valleys on either side were heavily wooded and would conceal the attacking aircraft until they turned over the spit to line up with the dam. Then the Lancasters would be cruelly exposed to flak guns, which as Harris feared would undoubtedly benefit from the beams of the Aldis lamps despite the efforts to mask them. The tops of the towers on the dam wall had been flattened and a single-barrelled 20mm flak gun capable of firing 120 rounds per minute installed on each. A third 20mm flak gun stood on a buttress towards the eastern end of the dam. All three could engage a aircraft virtually the whole distance from the Hever spit.

Below the Möhne Dam lay a large power station set among ornamental gardens, and a smaller power station on the western side of the equalising basin that helped to regulate the flow into the river as it ran towards the Ruhr. On rising ground close to the village of Günne to the north-east were three more flak guns in an ideal position to engage Lancasters that had crossed the dam and were turning to port after their attack. Fortunately there were no barrage balloons at this or any other target dam, and heavier flak guns had been withdrawn to defend the German cities.

The Möhne Dam: note the double anti-torpedo defences in the reservoir beyond the wall (top), the equalising basin (foreground), and the small power station (middle right). Three flak guns can just be made out by the crossroads at the bottom of the picture.

The Eder Dam: the Lancasters attacked from left to right over the reservoir. Note the two power stations below the dam wall.

The Sorpe Dam, with its different structure, lay six miles south-west of the Möhne. It was 600 metres (1965 feet) long and 58 metres (190 feet) high, and its 10-metre-wide concrete core was stabilised by earth banks covered with stone slabs, which sloped away on both the water and air sides. The reservoir, containing 72 million cubic metres of water, was lined with tree-covered hills. Attacking aircraft had to negotiate immediately to the west a hill 340 metres (1110 feet) high topped by the village of Langscheid; to the east the ground rose sharply to 324 metres (1060 feet). It was a difficult target, but at least there were no flak defences. Later the Air Staff explained that 'the intention was to cause leakage on a sufficient scale to force the Germans to empty the reservoir in order to effect repairs'. But Harris was right to argue that the chosen method of attack had scant chance of success, as he later recalled. 'I knew, and asserted from the start, that the Sorpe Dam was the wrong construction to collapse from the bouncing bomb, though there was a faint chance that it might start a leak, crack the concrete "blade" and then escaping water *might* do the rest.' The decision was made 'above my head'. Dick Collins, the Road Research Laboratory scientist, professed to being 'a little irritated' to learn that the Sorpe had been a target, 'because we could easily have made some model tests which I am sure could have made the attack more successful.'

The third Ruhr dam listed for attack was the Lister, close to the village of Attendorn and in hilly country fifty-five miles south-east of Duisburg. The 22 million cubic metres of water in its reservoir fed the Lenne tributary of the Ruhr River, and like the Möhne it curved into its reservoir. The ideal approach ran directly from the spit of land occupied by the village of Eichen to the west across 500 metres (545 yards) of open water, and there were no flak defences. There was, however, one major snag. The Lister Dam had only one central tower, whereas the British thought for some unexplained reason that it had two.

The final Ruhr target was the Ennepe Dam. Like the Möhne and Lister it curved in a convex manner into the reservoir, which had a capacity of 12.6 million cubic metres. Lying twenty miles due south of Dortmund and thirty miles south-west of the Möhne Dam, the Ennepe nestled in very hilly terrain with a most difficult approach run for an attacking aircraft. The dam was situated at the northern end of an irregular L-shaped reservoir. Midway between the towers, about 300 metres (327 yards) upstream, stood a tree-covered spit virtually astride the ideal bombing run. When the reservoir was full, as expected, this appeared on all maps as an island.

Of the two dams connected with the Weser Valley, the Eder was the bigger and more important. Similar to the Möhne, it was 399 metres (1309 feet) long, 42.4 metres (139 feet) high, 35 metres (115 feet) wide at the bottom, and 5.8 metres (19 feet) wide at the top, along which ran a road. It lay close to the village of Hemfurth and two miles south of Waldeck, whose castle was perched high above it. The reservoir, which contained 202 million cubic metres of water, snaked for about 7½ miles towards the Eder Dam, which lay twenty miles south-west of Kassel and fifty miles south-east of the Möhne. Below the dam wall, at its extremities, were two small power stations.

Confident that its geographical position offered ample protection, the Germans had no flak defences there. This did not seem foolhardy. The dam arched west-north-west into the reservoir, and immediately west of it stood a large tree-covered spit rising to 241 metres (790 feet). To the north the undulating terrain rose in places to 400 metres (1308 feet). Just 350 metres (381 yards) east (beyond) the dam, the height was 343 metres (1122 feet) – a challenging prospect for Lancasters crossing the dam and possibly still with 'Upkeep' on board. Nor was the approach run easy. The chosen method of attack was to dive over Waldeck Castle towards a point west of the spit in front of the dam, turning sharply to port and hopping over the spit to line up the final approach run.

The Diemel Reservoir (20 million cubic metres of water) lay twenty-two miles north-west of the Eder and thirty miles west of Kassel. Its dam, close to the village of Helminghausen, stood at the end of two narrow valleys, each approximately 3000 metres (3250 yards) long. From one of these, through which the Diemel River flowed, an aircraft would have an easy attacking run between two hills. But as with the Lister, the British falsely believed that there were two towers on the Diemel, when there were none. Fortunately, no crew had to contend with such an unexpected complication, for neither the Lister nor Diemel was attacked on the night.

At midday on 15 May Satterly instructed the 5 Group Chief Signals Officer, Wg Cdr W. E. Dunn, to study the Operation Order and devise appropriate wireless

Master and dog: Gibson, riding a power-assisted bicycle, with Nigger, who was killed on 15 May and buried at midnight the following day below Gibson's first-floor office.

schedules and procedures. As he did so, Cochrane made his way to Scampton to tell Whitworth and Gibson that Operation Chastise would take place the next day, Sunday 16 May.

Thorough maintenance checks were ordered for the eighteen serviceable 617 Lancasters. The special process to install 'Upkeep' required approximately half an hour per aircraft, so some did fly on 15 May. Barlow took Byers as his second pilot to Wainfleet for a bombing exercise, while Astell was among those to carry out an air test with his aircraft. Poignantly, none of these three pilots would survive the following night.

Just before 1600, Wallis touched down at Scampton in a Wellington flown by Summers. Two hours later he attended a meeting in Whitworth's house, where he and Gibson briefed the two fight commanders, Young and Maudslay, Hopgood, who would be Gibson's deputy at the Möhne Dam, and the Squadron's Australian bombing leader, Flt Lt R. C. (Bob) Hay. At that meeting Hopgood drew attention to a known defended area near Hüls not marked on the flak map, and the route was adjusted to avoid this hazard.

As the meeting broke up, Whitworth gave Gibson some distressing news. His dog, Nigger, had been run over and killed by a car outside the main gate. Wallis feared that this might be a dreadful omen. Gibson would the next morning ask Powell to ensure that Nigger's body was buried outside his first-floor office at midnight on 16 May.

So tight was the security that not even the adjutant knew about the target or that 617 Squadron would fly to the dams the next day. However, he sensed that something was afoot in the mess that evening, when he saw some officers unusually nursing soft drinks. Like many others, Grayston, Knight's flight engineer, went to sleep 'as normal', totally unaware of the impending operation, and had breakfast on 16 May still in ignorance.

On the Sunday morning unusual movements around the workshops, aircraft and bomb dump made it difficult to conceal that an operation was imminent, and Grayston soon picked up the signals. LAC Munro explained that 'the interaction between groundcrew and aircrew was such that your sixth sense told you that this was "it", by the way the crew acted.' Humphries agreed. In the 'general hive of activity, you couldn't escape the fact that they were going to do something. It was just an atmosphere.'

Shortly after the adjutant arrived at his office, Gibson came in to say, 'We're working tonight.' The adjutant asked which crews were flying, and Gibson replied that A and B flight commanders would let him have the list. Instead of 'the usual battle order', Gibson insisted that Humphries drew up a 'Night Flying Programme'. Grayston and other crew members soon learned that this was a subterfuge. Humphries duly printed the disguised programme, and distributed it to all sections including the messing section, which caused particular problems. Humphries had personally to visit the different messes, where 'unbelievably I had to sort of grovel' because the mess sergeants bluntly refused that evening to provide bacon and eggs, which were strictly reserved for pre-operational meals.

'Upkeep' in position: a close-up of the weapon on Gibson's Lancaster, AJ-G.

Having got over the hurdle of providing appropriate food, once he had the take-off times the adjutant arranged with the transport officer for the station buses to take aircrew out to their dispersal points. Among the many other tasks required to ensure that the operation went smoothly was the provision of an urn of tea when crews gathered at the flights to get their equipment. Humphries recorded that 'Gibson sort of disappeared and came back from time to time', and the station Tannoy called different members of 617 Squadron to the briefing room. Tracer was loaded into machine-guns, and armourers laboured to hoist 'Upkeep' into the aircraft so far without it. Before AJ-C was dealt with, Ottley took it up for an air test. He and all but one of his crew would be lost over Germany in the early hours of 17 May.

That afternoon an officer went into the machine shop in search of a grease gun, which Drury had modified for use with 'Upkeep'. Because Drury 'had been put to a great deal of trouble and had shown a great deal of patience', he took him to see one of the bombed-up Lancasters, telling him it would be his last chance to do so. In the hangar Drury saw 'what appeared to be a large steel drum hanging underneath the fuselage and a chain drive to revolve it in its bearing.' He had absolutely no idea what it was – another tribute to the tightness of security.

'Upkeep', the weapon that 617 Squadron would take to the dams, resembled a garden roller in its final version, rather than the large beer barrel originally intended. The cylinder, of ⅜-inch-thick metal, measured 59⅞ inches long by 50 inches in diameter and weighed 2250lb. Filled with 6600lb of Torpex underwater explosive compound, its total weight was 9250lb. Three hydrostatic pistols set to detonate 30 feet below the surface of the water, and the fourth self-destructive device, which would explode ninety seconds after release, were primed with Tetryl initiating explosive. The two V-shaped calliper arms protruded below the bomb-bay to hold 'Upkeep' firmly, and a 20-inch-diameter disc was mounted on the inside of their extremities to engage a track at each end of the 'Upkeep' cylinder. A belt linked to a Vickers hydraulic motor fixed above in the facing of the bomb-bay ran at forty-five degrees. As the Lancaster's hydraulic system was not required to operate the bomb-bay doors, which had been removed for this operation, a cut-out provision allowed diversion to the Vickers motor after the undercarriage had been raised. Using the valve of a compressor and an attached gauge, the wireless operator would regulate the back spin generated by this equipment. The bomb-aimer, apart from ensuring that 'Upkeep' was released at the right spot, operated the powerful springs that made the calliper arms spring outwards for the weapon to drop. While the flight engineer checked the speed of the aircraft, during the final approach the navigator would switch on the Aldis lamps and take his place at the Perspex blister to observe their relative positions.

With the exception of the Sorpe, at all other reservoirs crews were to attack at right-angles to the dam wall at precisely 220m.p.h. groundspeed, 60 feet altitude and with 'Upkeep' back-spinning at 500r.p.m. The weapon must be dropped between 425 and 475 yards from the target.

The Sorpe presented a different problem, and at a late date Wallis's idea of approaching it, like the other dams, at right-angles was abandoned. Instead, crews there were not to spin 'Upkeep', but were to fly along the top of the dam, line the port outer engine on the crest and drop 'Upkeep' in the middle. It would roll down the sloping support and explode 30 feet below the surface just like the others. It was hoped that the effect would be the same as with Wallis's rejected tactic: the shock wave would crack the central core, through which water would gradually seep to cause collapse.

Because of the unique nature of Operation Chastise, there was a series of briefings throughout the day, starting in late morning, with separate groups in different rooms. The hangars and offices were 'very quiet, like a morgue' to 'Chiefy' Powell. Gibson briefed the pilots and navigators before they dispersed separately to study the available information. Dunn, 5 Group Chief Signals Officer, travelled from Grantham similarly to talk to the wireless operators and give them special practice on a buzzer circuit. After about a couple of hours everybody broke for refreshment, but remained tight-lipped. The remaining crew members were told nothing, and Tees, Ottley's rear

The Möhne Dam briefing model: the aircraft flew from right to left along the lower river, turned over the spit (centre) and attacked the dam (bottom right).

gunner, consoled himself with the thought, 'Well, it can't be any worse than others [raids].' Sutherland, Knight's front gunner, had a similar experience: 'On the day of the raid, they called the pilots and navigators and they had their briefing of what was, where it was and which aircraft were where. The rest of the crew still didn't know, and we said, "What did you learn?" They said, "We can't tell you, you'll have to wait until tonight when there's another briefing."'

Throughout the afternoon those already briefed returned to study the models of the Möhne and Sorpe dams prepared by RAF Medmenham (incredibly, that of the Eder was not completed until the morning after the operation), charts, still photographs and other data that had been collated in target files.

As all of this was taking place, the Air Ministry stressed that, to ensure consistency, post-operational communiqués should be only released by it, not by Bomber Command, 5 Group, or RAF Scampton. The press would be given details in accordance with a cover story agreed on 25 March: 'A mine of great size' had been dropped by crews 'specially and rigorously trained' for a task 'which demanded an extraordinarily high standard of flying and the highest degree of accuracy in dropping of the mines sufficiently close to the target to be effective.'

Meteorological forecasts were favourable, so no last-minute postponement would be necessary. At 1645 a cypher message was sent by 5 Group to Scampton: 'Execute Operation Chastise 16/5/43 zero hour 2248'. The way was now open for all members of the crews (including the gunners and flight engineers so far in the dark) to gather for what Martin's rear gunner Simpson called 'the longest briefing I ever attended'. Due to sickness, only nineteen crews were scheduled to fly that night.

The Sorpe Dam briefing model: the aircraft flew from left to right along the dam (top centre). Langscheid village with its prominent church spire is to the left of the dam, the reservoir in the centre, and the rectangular equalising basin at the top.

In the upstairs briefing room, at 1800, all aircrew 'noisily assembled'. After the squadron and other 'necessary people' were inside, the door was locked. Nevertheless, an interloper did gain access. During the afternoon, Longbottom and Handasyde had flown the trial Wellington to Scampton, and Herbert Jeffree from Wallis's staff had hitched a lift. Seeing that 'a flap was on and tight security about to close the station', the two pilots rapidly took off again, leaving Jeffree behind. Hearing that a briefing was in progress, he showed a pass that authorised attendance at Manston and Reculver, but certainly not at that final briefing. He had never attended one before and rather fancied the experience. Boldness was rewarded, and the sentry let him in. As he took a seat at the back, Gibson was telling the crews that they were going to attack 'the great dams of Germany', the overture to a short pep talk, which made a lasting impression on Sutherland. 'If you don't do it tonight, you're going back tomorrow night,' he could recall above all else.

Then staff officers ran over details of Operation Order B.976 (much of it familiar to pilots, navigators and wireless operators). Immediately opposite the door, senior officers were on a raised platform with their backs to the window. Crews were told that the industrial Ruhr relied 'to a very large extent on enormously costly water barrage dams', and destruction of the Möhne 'alone would bring about a serious shortage of water for drinking purposes and industrial supplies'. The 'additional destruction of one or more of the five major dams in the Ruhr area would greatly increase the effect and hasten the resulting damage' – the Sorpe Dam being 'next in importance'. 'Substantial' damage, 'considerable local flooding' and 'a large loss of electrical capacity' through destruction of hydro-electricity stations and denial of cooling water for the thermal plants 'might well cause havoc in the Ruhr Valley'. Further east, 'in the Weser District', destruction of the Eder Dam 'would seriously hamper transport in the Mittelland Canal and in the Weser [River], and would probably lead to an almost complete cessation of the great volume of traffic now using these waterways.' The distinction between the Ruhr and the Weser areas was therefore clear.

Referring to a cross-sectional drawing of the Möhne Dam and occasionally using a blackboard, Wallis explained the construction and characteristics of each target dam. He went on to outline how 'Upkeep' had been developed and how it worked. In underlining the importance of water for German industry, he noted that eight tons were needed to produce every ton of steel. He believed that the squadron had the means to strike a blow from which the Germans would not recover 'for a very long time'. Because the Kaiser had personally opened the Möhne in 1913, to general amusement he observed that it must be a prime target. There were, though, few moments of light relief. Wallis made a 'lasting impression' on George Chalmers, Townsend's wireless operator, while Jim Clay, Munro's bomb-aimer, found his explanation 'detailed and clear'. Clay added that 'it seemed incongruous that this kindly and quietly spoken man should be involved with devastation.' The American Joe McCarthy agreed that he seemed 'a genial man'.

After Wallis, Cochrane spoke. He felt sure that the crews would do 'a tremendous amount of damage', and prophetically that the operation would be 'historic'. He stressed the need for absolute secrecy after the operation, as Wallis's weapon was destined for use on other targets. He did not reveal that a smaller version was already being developed for attacks on German and Italian capital ships, including *Tirpitz*. 'I know this attack will succeed,' Cochrane concluded, and after he sat down Gibson rose to summarise operational details.

The nineteen aircraft would be divided into three waves. He would lead the first, comprising nine aircraft divided into three formations of three, taking off at intervals of ten minutes. This wave would fly what became known as 'the southern route', crossing the North Sea to make landfall in the Scheldt estuary before skirting the main German defences and attacking the Möhne Dam (Target X). There Gibson would co-ordinate the individual attacks via R/T. Wallis hoped that one 'Upkeep' would be sufficient, but cautious staff officers thought three would be necessary. Once the Möhne had been destroyed, the remaining aircraft of that wave would fly to the Eder Dam (Target Y), where Gibson would direct 'similar tactics'. Any Lancasters still with 'Upkeep' after these two dams had been destroyed would attack the Sorpe (Target Z).

By then the Sorpe should have been hit by the so-called Second Wave, though this would actually take off before Gibson. Flying individually, with McCarthy in the lead, five Lancasters were to take 'the northern route' across the North Sea to the island of Vlieland in the Frisian chain off the Dutch coast, then turn south-east over the Ijsselmeer (Zuider Zee) to join the southern route in the area of the German border. The earlier take-off of these aircraft would ensure that both the First and Second Waves would cross the Dutch coast approximately 120 miles apart at the same time and possibly fool the Germans into thinking that they were minor nuisance incursions. The fourteen aircraft of the First and Second Waves would get airborne at about 2300 (9.30pm, Double British Summer Time).

The remaining five Lancasters were to form a Mobile Reserve, ready to attack the Möhne, Eder or Sorpe dams, if any had not been breached, or the other three, the Lister (D), Ennepe (E) or Diemel (F). They would take off at about midnight (2½ hours after the others), and be directed to their targets while in the air via a W/T (wireless telegraphy) link with 5 Group.

If one 'Upkeep' accounted for each of the Möhne and Eder dams, seven aircraft from the First Wave could go to the Sorpe in addition to the five Second Wave Lancasters sent directly to it, which incidentally disproves later criticism that the importance of the Sorpe was not recognised. Because aircraft of the Mobile Reserve might also be ordered to the Sorpe, all crews were briefed on the different method of attack there, as well as that on the five gravity dams.

Aircraft were not to exceed 1500 feet over England, then were to descend to 60 feet over the North Sea to test their Aldis lamps and remain at low level (100 feet) to the target area at a speed of 180m.p.h. The need to keep low was dictated by the slow speed, which would make the aircraft vulnerable to night-fighters and heavy flak at a higher altitude. The Operation Order, written by Satterly, laid down that aircraft should remain at low level after leaving the target area until reaching 03 degrees 00 minutes E. Three return routes, between which individual aircraft were distributed, had been drawn up for the Lancasters to cross the Helder peninsula, west of the Zuider Zee, at different places. Crews flying back were warned to cross the enemy coast 'at the lowest possible height', then maintain a maximum height of 500 feet until the English coast.

Wireless procedures included important codewords, such as 'Nigger' for the breaching of the Möhne, and 'Dinghy' for the Eder. 'Cooler', followed by the appropriate number, would be used on R/T during the operation to identify individual aircraft. 'Goner' would signify release of an 'Upkeep' with a figure added to denote its effect: 1, failed to explode; 2, overshot the dam; 3, exploded more than 100 yards from the dam; 4, exploded 100 yards from the dam; 5, exploded 50 yards from the dam; 6, exploded 5 yards from the dam; 7, exploded in contact with the dam; 8, no apparent breach; 9, small breach; 10, large breach. For signalling purposes the Möhne, Eder and Sorpe dams became A, B and C respectively. So '710A' transmitted to Grantham would indicate that 'Upkeep' had exploded in contact with the Möhne and caused a large breach. At the Sorpe, where the unspun 'Upkeep' would be dropped from the 'lowest possible height', a red Very cartridge would be fired as each aircraft released its weapon. At all other dams it would be fired as the Lancaster crossed the dam, that is after releasing the weapon.

As the crews were about to dismiss, Sutherland explained that Gibson 'said you can all file up to the front of the room and see the mock-up of these dams. It was really scary to see the dams and the Möhne Dam had the flak towers and it just looked really rough. After a while you got a feeling like you were going to Essen, which with its 50,000 flak guns you know it's tough. But this one seemed to be worse, it just seemed to be the ultimate in dangerous things to do, so I was scared, really scared.' The padre, Revd C. D. Hulbert, later revealed that after the briefing one of the aircrew went to him 'very stressed' and asked for Hulbert's special support.

Longbottom's aircraft was not the only one to land at Scampton that afternoon. Because the Lancaster damaged by Maudslay at Reculver could not be repaired, only nineteen aircraft were available for nineteen crews – no reserve in case of a last-minute emergency. Two of the three Type 464 Provisioning Lancasters allocated for trial purposes were still at Manston; the third was at Boscombe Down, and Commander H. C. Bergel of No. 9 Ferry Pilots Pool was detailed to fly it up to Scampton. He looked in astonishment at the 'gutted fish', without bomb-bay doors or a mid-upper turret, and two metal arms with small wheels at their extremities dangling underneath. The driving belt attached to the hydraulic motor bolted to the cabin floor was also a mystery. He had no time to linger, though. Testing the engines before take-off, he identified a malfunction of the fuel booster pump for No. 3 engine, but in view of the urgency of the situation decided to 'ignore' this. Arriving at Scampton at about 1530, he noticed more 'gutted' Lancasters around the perimeter carrying objects 'about the size and shape of the front wheel of a steam roller', one of which was slowly rotating.

Above The crew of AJ-G preparing for take-off: (left to right) Flt Lt R. D. Trevor Roper, Sgt J. Pulford, F/Sgt G. A. Deering, Plt Off F. M. Spafford, Flt Lt R. E. G. Hutchison, Gibson, and Plt Off H. T. Taerum.

Left Last-minute adjustments: Gibson (right) and Hutchison, his navigator who flew with him on 106 Squadron.

He set off to investigate, only to be swiftly intercepted and sharply told to stay clear. Anxious not to be confined to the station, Bergel rapidly withdrew to a waiting Anson. 'I had no idea what this peculiarly modified aeroplane was required to do, and it was made clear that curiosity was most unwelcome.' Nobody ever told him that, without his delivery that afternoon, 617 Squadron would have flown only eighteen Lancasters to the dams.

After the briefing the crews had their evening meal, and the presence of two eggs on each plate (the traditional pre-operational menu) alerted waitresses and two WAAF intelligence officers – one of whom would marry the Australian pilot David Shannon – to the impending action. Arthurton, the medical officer, asked Shannon's rear gunner, Fg Off Jack Buckley, if he could fly on that night's exercise and received an evasive answer. An NCO who made an indiscreet remark in the Sergeants' Mess was instantly rebuked by his fellows. Security was still tight.

Clay believed that 'everyone was in high spirits and ready to go', which was far from true. Detailed to attack the Sorpe, Rice was worried about having to 'wriggle around' the church steeple at Langscheid and dropping 'Upkeep' at low speed without spinning. Diving over the steep hill on which the village stood meant having to put the flaps down for the attack run. Townsend, a Mobile Reserve pilot, felt physically sick, convinced they were 'all for the chop'. O'Brien, Knight's Canadian rear gunner, noted how some crew members huddled quietly talking around tables; others joked nervously in loud voices. Hopgood told Shannon he thought that he wouldn't come back, and this would prove a sadly accurate prediction. Young tided his room; many wrote letters to their relatives. More boisterous spirits went out to see the monster cylinders attached to their aircraft. Sgt Basil Feneron, Brown's flight engineer, tried to lift it; Warrant Officer A. A. Garshowitz, Astell's Canadian wireless operator, chalked on his 'Upkeep': 'Never has so much been expected of so few.' Astell's Lancaster would be shot down.

The ninety minutes before take-off were always a tense time on any station, but the long preparation for this unusual operation made it even more testing. 'This was Der Tag for 617 Squadron,' the adjutant recorded. 'From eight o'clock onwards the scenes outside the crew rooms were something to behold.' Crews converged on the squadron hangar to collect parachutes and other equipment, some then lounged on the grass in the late evening sun, others commandeered deck chairs, and a few hardy souls played cricket. Gibson arrived with his whole crew packed into his car, radiating confidence. He went across to Humphries, reminding him to have beer ready for their return. Gibson was 'fit and well and quite unperturbed,' Humphries wrote. Later Gibson would admit to concealing his qualms – the leadership qualities, which Howard and Humphries both highlighted.

Soon the time came to move, and men and equipment were piled into the buses and trucks that would ferry them to the dispersal points and their aircraft. Many, like O'Brien, saw 'Upkeep' for the first time and marvelled at its strange shape; to Johnson (McCarthy's bomb-aimer) it was 'a large cylindrical dustbin'. As they made their way to the hard stand, in an effort to lighten the tension, his rear gunner (Buckley) mischievously asked Shannon, 'Have you cleaned your teeth?' Members of the First and Second Wave crews soon climbed aboard for final pre-flights tests, though not before some had superstitiously performed personal rituals. Whittaker watered the tail wheel of Martin's aircraft, Martin himself tucked a toy koala bear into his jacket. The Canadian pilot Ken Brown smoked two cigarettes, while Howard completed a ritual walk round the outside of Townsend's Lancaster. Once the checks had been completed, captains shut down the engines and 'the worst half-hour of the day' began. The operation might yet be called off.

Shortly after 2100 Gibson's wireless operator, Hutchison, fired the red Very light for engines to be restarted and pilots to move on to the perimeter track in preparation for take-off. At 2128 a green light flashed from the control caravan and the aircraft of the Australian Flt Lt R. N. G. Barlow slowly gathered speed northwards along the runway of RAF Scampton, a 'thrilling sight' to Humphries. Operation Chastise had begun.

Crews of the Mobile Reserve, administrative staff, groundcrew and civilian workers like Jeffree watched Barlow go. As the Lancaster gradually hauled itself off the grass, Jeffree noted what a long run the laden aircraft needed to get airborne against the background of a beautiful sunset. The Vickers-Armstrongs' scientist reflected that his work was now finished; that of the 617 crews was about to begin. Officially, nobody but a privileged few outside the squadron knew that they were off on their long-awaited attack. But Powell thought 'the whole station was there to see them off', because it was clearly 'a death or glory job'.

When the last of the First and Second Wave aircraft had disappeared from view, the five Mobile Reserve (Third Wave) Lancaster crews drifted away. Two hours of uncertainty lay ahead. Several played cards, rolled dice or dozed. Convinced that he could not survive such a hair-raising business, Doug Webb, Townsend's front gunner, went for a bath, 'determined to die clean'.

Section III

Crashes and Successes

Training on the Simulator

**'Don't listen to them, listen to the Nav! We are our own army! We are our own army!...
Aaah, we've crashed...'**

Branty

None of the crew expected much of the Simulator, thinking it would just be a bigger version of the desk-top Sims they used at Cranwell on a daily basis for practice. They were in for a surprise. During the training Kenji Takeda and his team at the University of Southampton had been adapting Microsoft's Flightsim to take software for the Lancaster controls made by Cambridgeshire based software experts Just Flight. He had stretched the software to its limit with customised scenery and a work station for each crew member.

At the Meridian Studios in Southampton a team of carpenters had been building a life-size skeleton of a Lancaster (with one side open so that the crew could be seen cramped inside). Jeremy Hall, a VAT inspector who happens to own a Lancaster fuselage, loaned the production the unique pilot's seat, navigator's seat and table, radios and control panels. Once simulator expert Takeda had connected each work station to the computers, the crew would be able to fly the Lancaster across Europe and drop a bouncing bomb on their target. Four vast screens curving around the Simulator showed the terrain in detail. These were the finishing touches to the

The ergonomically accurate Lancaster frame of the simulator.

machine. Once the studio lights were down, the monitors and giant screens immersed the crew, and the sound of the roaring Merlin engines drowned all other contact with the ground. They felt as close as possible to the mind-set of the AJ-N Dambusters crew sixty years before them.

Each crew position was covered by a camera linked to a monitor and recorder in the control room – the nerve centre of the operation. The crew could talk to each other on the intercom – essential with the sound of four screaming Merlin engines around them. The communications system allowed the pilot to talk to other aircraft and the Wireless Operator to talk back to England (actually the control room, where banks of monitors allowed Frankie and the crew's real-life Squadron Leader to monitor progress, picking up mistakes and planning de-briefs and new missions). Short of physically taking off and flying to Germany there was nothing the simulator couldn't do.

The film-makers had everything down to the last detail. But in reality they were more apprehensive than the crew. Would the simulator handle like a real Lancaster? And would the software – stretched to its limits – survive a six-hour mission without crashing?

At least there was relief when the crew saw the Simulator for the first time – they were amazed and delighted, even though some had very uncomfortable positions. Molly would have to lie down in a space barely 2 feet high in the Bomb Aimer's position (just as E. C. 'Johnny' Johnson had sixty years before him) with Teri sitting virtually on top of him as Front Gunner. Impressed with what they had seen so far, the crew filed into the briefing room to hear about their first training flight.

Frankie had drawn the short straw in the crew lottery: he had to understudy each role so that he could stand in as a reserve in

Lucy in the pilot's seat.

Branty navigating.

Molly looks for landmarks.

case anyone fell ill or had an accident. But he also had the task of planning the training missions and acting as controller while they were flying. At best he was going to be unpopular; at worst he might get saddled with Branty's Navigator's job.

The first mission was flown in the daytime at 3000 feet over England. The crew got lost. The second mission was flown at night at 250 feet. Lost again, the crew finally managed to find its target of Derwent Water, but three attempts to line up on the dam for a target run were complete failures. On the third mission the crew got completely confused over the North Yorkshire Moors but recovered when they stumbled across the A1. Finally finding Derwent Water they took three runs on to the dam and hit it on the third attempt.

Intense practice was now called for. In order to hit a dam and destroy it the aircraft must fly at exactly 230 miles per hour (knots were not used until after the Second World War) at a height of 60 feet. Only then can the bomb be released between 300 and 400 yards from the dam wall. Lucy the Pilot was in control of the direction, Tapper the Flight Engineer the speed, Branty the Navigator controlled the height by looking out at the two spotlights on the water, and Molly the Bomb Aimer controlled the distance and was in charge of when and if to release the bomb. It was an extremely testing piece of teamwork, especially in an age where the work of all these people is largely done by computer. But it was soon clear to everyone present in the control room, including acting commander Frankie, that the human computers were improving.

Navigation no longer scared the crew but did always demand their constant attention. At the cost of his popularity Frankie had changed the way the Lancaster was flown by changing the Sim

Teri looks through the gunsight.

The bank of monitors in the control room.

The crew watch their own performance.

set-up with Kenji – a result of his after-hours practising. The plane was now more difficult to fly, but also more like the real thing. The team took off for some solid target practice at Ladybower Reservoir. After eight runs they hit the target four times, two hits on the last two runs. Encouraged by a little success and tired of the control room's constant monitoring and advice, the crew got a little over-confident:

'They're giving us advice but it's the same as what we're doing!'

'Don't listen to them, listen to the Nav! We are our own army! We are our own army!… Aaah, we've crashed…'

With all the distraction 60 feet had become zero feet. They had crashed and burned without even noticing what was happening. Andy the Wireless Operator summed it all up: 'Bad news, but we blew up the dam and won a posthumous Victoria Cross.' Despite the crash and Andy's irony, skills had actually

Molly, Tapper, Lucy and Branty in Canada – in modern gear (below) and in WWII uniforms (opposite).

improved greatly – if only the crew could start taking it as seriously as they needed to.

Tapper, Lucy, Branty and Molly then flew to Canada to experience flying in a real Lancaster at the Canadian Warplane Heritage Museum. The Pilot, Don Schoffield, used to be in the Royal Canadian Air Force; his first station commander was Dambusters pilot Joe McCarthy. The Lancaster came to life in the air in a way no simulator really can, a vibrating mass surrounded by the noise of the four twelve-cylinder engines throbbing in and out of phase. Qualified pilots Lucy and Branty took the controls for a few minutes and were blown away by the experience. Molly couldn't believe he had actually had the opportunity to fly in a Lancaster. All had a lump in their throats while flying in this cultural icon. And riding with them was Ray Grayston, the Flight Engineer of AJ-N for Nan, astonishingly flying in a Lancaster for the first time since he baled out of one

Being shown the weapons.

Final instruction before take-off.

The Chinook takes to the air.

Heading out over The Wash.

Al takes aim.

Target practice.

at 80 feet in September 1943: 'It's terrifying in the back. I'd rather be up in the front working – keeps your mind off it.' Spending time with Ray in Canada, flying on the real McCoy and talking to the pilots who flew the plane in Canada all helped to inform the crew's understanding of what it took for these groups of seven men to climb aboard for mission after mission throughout the war.

Meanwhile the Air Gunners, Al and Teri, were learning the equivalent role in the modern RAF. They flew in a Chinook helicopter to firing ranges in the Wash. The M60 7.62mm machine-gun has a rate of fire similar to the .30 Browning machine-guns used in the Lancaster turrets. Teri and Al fired at ship hulks from the rear of the helicopter, watching the tracer bullets lazily arc towards the ground as the cabin filled with the smell of cordite. Up front was another, more formidable weapon. The M134 minigun fires an incredible 66 rounds of 7.62mm ammunition a second, giving it firepower that AJ-N Gunners Fred Sutherland and Harry O'Brien could only have dreamed of.

The crew re-grouped in Southampton for their last Simulator training missions in a more sober mood. The more they had learned about the skills of sixty years ago the more they found themselves coming together as a team. To test them further, the control room decided that their aircraft would be damaged by anti-aircraft fire. Lucy, as aircraft captain, really showed her true colours when under pressure from the rest of the crew to bale out. She decided to ditch the plane in the English Channel, thus keeping everyone together with a better hope of survival and rescue, where baling would have left them all as singletons. This mission was followed by more bombing practice. There was now an almost tangible and very noticeable difference in the professionalism of the new crew. The next time they flew together would be on the same mission as that flown by AJ-N back in 1943 on the Dambusters raids.

But AJ-N had become a cohesive crew over many operational flights. Could the new crew really hope to emulate them?

CHAPTER

8

Möhne and Eder Dams

First Wave Attacks

At 2139, after a sweltering day, while the sun still hovered over the western horizon and a ghostly moon formed in the east, with Hopgood on his right in AJ-M and Martin on his left in AJ-P, Gibson slowly began to roll Lancaster AJ-G up the grass runway of RAF Scampton. The sight of three bombers taking off together was distinctly unusual. Weighed down by the strange object hanging below their fuselages, which caused Gibson to dub his aircraft 'a pregnant duck', like Barlow before them the first aircraft of the First Wave barely managed to haul themselves over the perimeter hedge.

After leaving Scampton they flew south-eastwards across the Wash and the familiar Wainfleet bombing range towards Southwold, where they crossed the English coast on schedule a little under forty minutes after take-off. Martin's navigator Leggo found his compass reading had a five-degree error and thereafter made the necessary adjustment. He would not be the only navigator to have a troublesome compass that night.

Over the calm North Sea all three Lancasters tested their spotlights successfully, but Gibson experienced difficulty with his automatic pilot, which he eventually ignored. The stronger winds than forecast found them to starboard of the planned track, so that they reached the enemy coast late and in the wrong place. Instead of turning in the mouth of the Scheldt between Schouwen and Walcheren islands, they made landfall on Walcheren, which was heavily defended. Fortunately, the enemy gunners failed to react there or when they flew over South Beveland, rapidly changing course towards Roosendaal. Gibson climbed to 300 feet to identify the anticipated windmill and wireless masts, so that his navigator, Taerum, could plot the new bearing. Meanwhile, the three bomb-aimers carried out initial arming of the self-destructive device in 'Upkeep'.

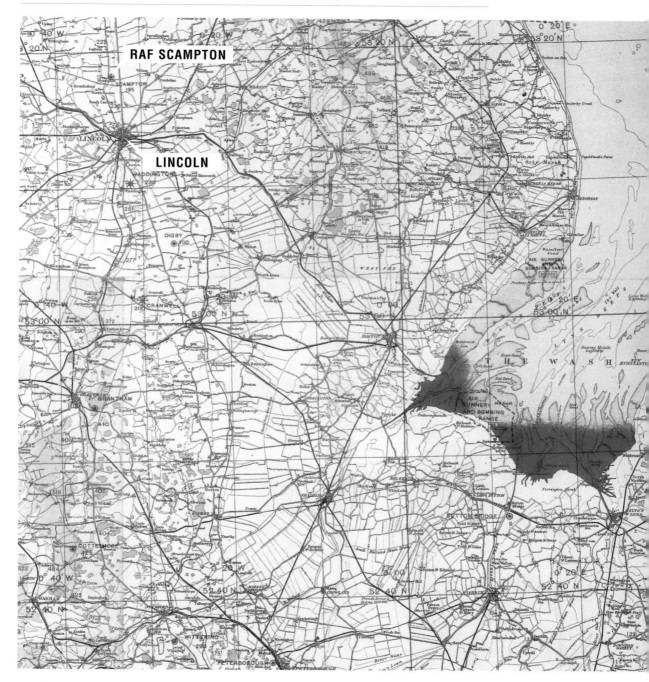

RAF SCAMPTON

LINCOLN

Gibson's bomb-aimer, Spafford, used a special roller, in his skipper's words rather like 'a roll of lavatory paper', for following the terrain on joined-up maps. He could therefore help Taerum identify salient features and avoid dangerous obstacles such as overhead power lines as they flew on at 100 feet. From Roosendaal the Lancasters made for a prominent railway intersection sixteen miles west of Breda, then almost due east

Take-off: after leaving Scampton, six miles north of Lincoln, the aircraft of the First Wave flew south-east across The Wash towards Southwold on the North Sea coast.

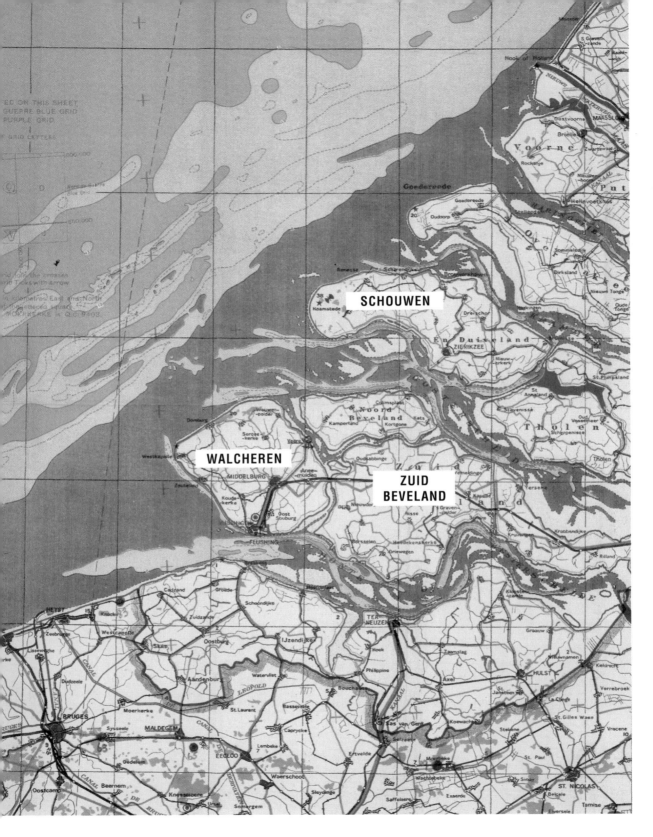

to pick up the Wilhelmina Canal, which ran conveniently between the fighter airfields of Gilze-Rijen to port and Eindhoven to starboard. At Beek the canal met another at right-angles, and from there the formation progressed unmolested to the Rhine, where the aircraft realised that they were again off track, six miles too far south. Banking sharply to port, Gibson made for the scheduled alteration of course at the bend of the river near Rees, and for the first time the Lancasters came under fire when flak barges on the river and static positions on the banks opened up.

The three reached Rees without damage, and turned east towards the next reference point, the lakes near Dülmen. Once more the aircraft drifted off track, proving how difficult it was to navigate at such a low altitude. In addition, unexpected pockets of resistance were encountered. They ran into a concentration of light (20mm and 37mm) flak supported by an estimated fifty searchlights in the Bocholt-Borken area. North-west of Dorsten all three Lancasters were coned by searchlights and fired on. East of Dülmen light flak damaged Hopgood's port wing and was so fierce that at 0007 Gibson's wireless operator broke radio silence to warn 5 Group of its location, information that was re-broadcast to airborne 617 aircraft four minutes later. Shortly after this Hopgood's aircraft sank so low to avoid flak that the Australian rear gunner, Plt Off A. F. Burcher, looked up to see it going under high-tension wires. Skirting the defended marshalling yards of Hamm to the north, Gibson flew on to the last turning point, the junction of several railway lines near Ahlen. Flying south between Werl and Soest, AJ-G at length breasted a tree-covered range of hills and looked down on the moon-drenched Möhne Reservoir.

A post-operational summary rather sparingly described the experiences of Gibson's trio en route to the Möhne. 'Various small flak posts opened up and as the aircraft flew over a defended area they were caught in the beam of searchlights while flying at a very low level, but their low level and high speed helped them escape from the searchlights and flak. Several searchlights were shot out of action.' This account did not mention the navigational problems, which caused the three Lancasters to reach the Möhne separately. Simpson, Martin's rear gunner, wrote in his diary: 'Lost Hoppy! Later picked up by some searchlights near Rhine – shot some out somewhere – bit off track over some town – bags of shooting – lost Winco – arrived Möhne, Hoppy and Winco turned up.'

The second formation in the First Wave left Scampton at 2147, led by Young flying AJ-A, with Maltby in AJ-J on his right and Shannon in AJ-L to the left. These three Lancasters would follow the southern route in Gibson's wake. They reached the Scheldt estuary accurately and all armed the self-destructive device shortly after crossing the coast. Just short of Roosendaal, long before Gibson's aircraft had come under fire, they took 'evasive action' to avoid flak. Maltby's navigator, Sgt V. Nicholson, noted that Young turned too soon at Beek and that 'Gee [was] jammed something chronic' fifteen miles from the Rhine. Three more times, near Dülmen, Ludinghausen and Ahlen, Maltby had to take evasive action, reaching the Möhne at 0026.

Opposite Landfall: the Lancasters were to turn over the Scheldt estuary between the islands of Schouwen and Walcheren, but off-track Gibson crossed Walcheren and South ('Zuid') Beveland.

Shannon's bomb-aimer, Sumpter, did not use the roller system like Spafford with Gibson, preferring to fold his 1:250,000 maps with the high-tension wires specially highlighted, which in practice he had no difficulty in identifying. Reasoning that there was no point trying to bale out at treetop height, Sumpter did not wear a parachute harness. To the consternation of the other two pilots, who made their feelings known by signalling lamps, Young persisted in flying too high (though still only about 500 feet). Again, navigation was a problem. Shannon arrived at the Möhne after the other two, to be 'hosepiped' by flak as he flew over the right-hand tower.

The third formation of Gibson's wave ran into more trouble than the others and lost one Lancaster. Led by Maudslay flying AJ-Z, with Astell in AJ-B and Knight in AJ-N to the right and left respectively, it took off from Scampton at 2159. Sutherland, Knight's front gunner, recalled that there was 'a little shack [actually a caravan] on the edge of the runway rather than the control tower and there was a guy in there with a green light. The three of us all lined up and when we got the green light we revved up and all went down the runway together. It was a hell of a long run because we had so much weight.' He reflected that 'once you get in the aircraft no matter how scared you are before or how apprehensive you are once you start down the runway, well then it's okay, you're committed and what happens, happens.' Apart from his general qualms about the operation after the briefing, like many others that evening Sutherland had worried about getting off the grass runway.

The three Lancasters reached the Scheldt estuary slightly behind schedule at 2321, due to the stronger winds and the need to adjust for a two-degree drift to starboard. Unlike the other aircraft, AJ-N armed its self-destructive device as it crossed the English coast at Southwold at 2248. Over the Continent, AJ-N's navigator Hobday praised 'the excellent route … with its recognisable turning points and short distance between them'. In the rear turret, O'Brien noticed that in the bright moonlight 'farm houses, some people, rivers, canals, roads, haystacks, gun positions were easily seen'. Sutherland also commented on the 'very bright moonlight, though your eyes were accustomed to seeing in the dark, especially rivers and fields. But you couldn't see any detail in the distance. There'd be a gun go off at the side of you and you wouldn't know it was there. Maybe in daylight you could have seen some movement or a gun, but at night you can't. You can't get that detail, so they've got first shot and that's where you know you haven't got much of a hope if they were any good. If they're accurate, well you're gone. But once they shoot and they don't hit you, well you've got hope.' Grayston, the flight engineer, was confident that at such low level they would have no trouble from fighters, because 'below 150 feet they couldn't pick you up on radar'.

In the bomb-aimer's position, Johnson carried out, in his own words, 'super map reading' with the roller system, passing visual information up to Hobday to assist him in plotting the course. Unlike other navigators, Hobday had 'extraordinarily good Gee' over the Continent beyond normal range. Sutherland thought the high tension wires a particular problem: 'Everybody kind of co-operated to say there's something there that we have to avoid. We always went over them and they were high. It took a long time to get up and over. I was so scared, I guess.' Apart from these obstacles, Johnson and O'Brien agreed that for AJ-N there was 'no real trouble – some flak, some searchlights'. That did not apply to Astell.

Between the turning points at Rees and Dülmen, AJ-B crashed. It seemed to hesitate at an intermediate pinpoint and turned after the other two. Knight's wireless operator, Kellow, looking back through the astrodome, witnessed Astell's fate as he strove to catch the others. He saw flak guns open up on AJ-B from both sides, creating a deadly crossfire. Although both of Astell's gunners responded strongly, the aircraft did not survive. It flew on for a short distance, then eight miles north-west of Dorsten the Lancaster became engulfed in flames and exploded when it hit the ground.

At 0020, about the time that Astell crashed, Martin crested the ridge to the north of the Möhne Reservoir. When Hopgood and Gibson joined him shortly afterwards, the Squadron Commander thought how 'grey and solid ... squat and heavy and unconquerable' the dam looked in the moonlight. The briefing had been accurate: there were no balloons and the flak positions on the towers, dam wall and in a meadow close to the village of Günne were identified, though such was their rate of fire that up to twelve guns were reported. The other crews heard Gibson say, 'Stand by chaps, I'm going to look the place over.' AJ-G flew through the lattice of shells unharmed; turning to port, it flew back along the Heve River and Gibson said that he 'liked the look of it'. Walker, Shannon's Canadian navigator, reflected that the flak would be 'beautiful in all its colours' if it had not been so lethal.

There were two bridges over the Möhne (right) sleeve of the reservoir, and the planned tactic was to dive over the further of those at Körbecke to gain the necessary speed. Each aircraft would then fly along the Möhne River and clear the Hevers Berg spit to line up its attack about 1500 metres (just under a mile) from the dam wall. This manoeuvre was complicated by the fact that the spit of land was to the right of an ideal approach run. The open nature of the last stretch of water meant that the three flak guns on the wall, having been depressed, could engage each Lancaster head-on as it strove to find the correct height, speed and spot to release 'Upkeep'.

Over the R/T Gibson warned the others to be ready to attack, and Hopgood to take over as leader should he be shot down. As AJ-G made its final approach at 230m.p.h. the flight engineer, navigator and bomb-aimer carried out their allotted tasks and the Canadian F/Sgt G. A. Deering in the front turret sprayed the wall's defences. Watching from afar, Shannon's crew saw the enemy fire intensify as Gibson got closer to the dam. But for the second time AJ-G crossed the dam wall safely, this time after releasing 'Upkeep' at 0028 in 'bright moon, no cloud, very good visibility'. Looking back, Flt Lt R. D. Trevor Roper, in the rear turret, saw the weapon bounce three times and, after a delay of about ten seconds, noted a tremendous sheet of water surge upwards after 'a terrific explosion'. He felt sure that the dam had been breached. When the water subsided, though, clearly it had not been destroyed. Hutchison signalled 'Goner 68A' – 'Upkeep' exploded 5-50 yards from the dam without breaching it.

Into Germany: all three waves would turn near Rees to skirt north of the industrial Ruhr. Of the First Wave, Astell was shot down near Borken on the way in, and Maudslay near Emmerich on the way back. Barlow, of the Second Wave, was lost near Rees itself.

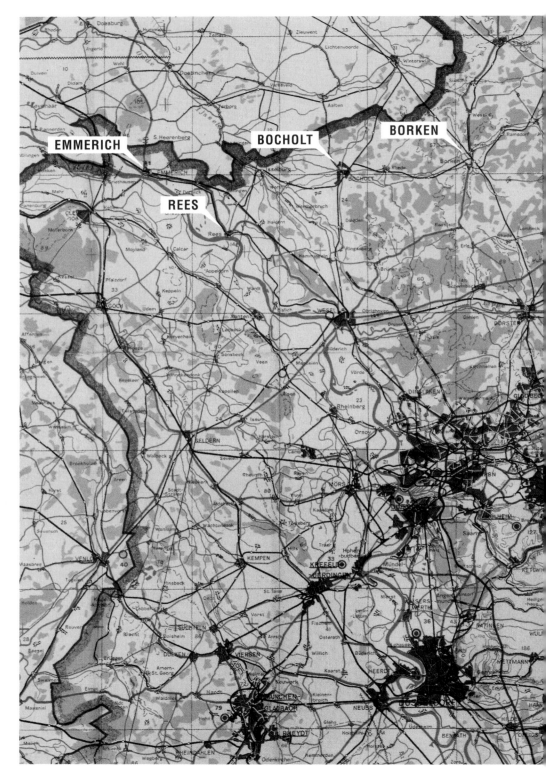

EMMERICH

BOCHOLT

BORKEN

REES

Opposite Final approach: from the prominent lakes near Dülmen, the aircraft made for Ahlen, then flew between Werl and Soest to the Möhne Dam.

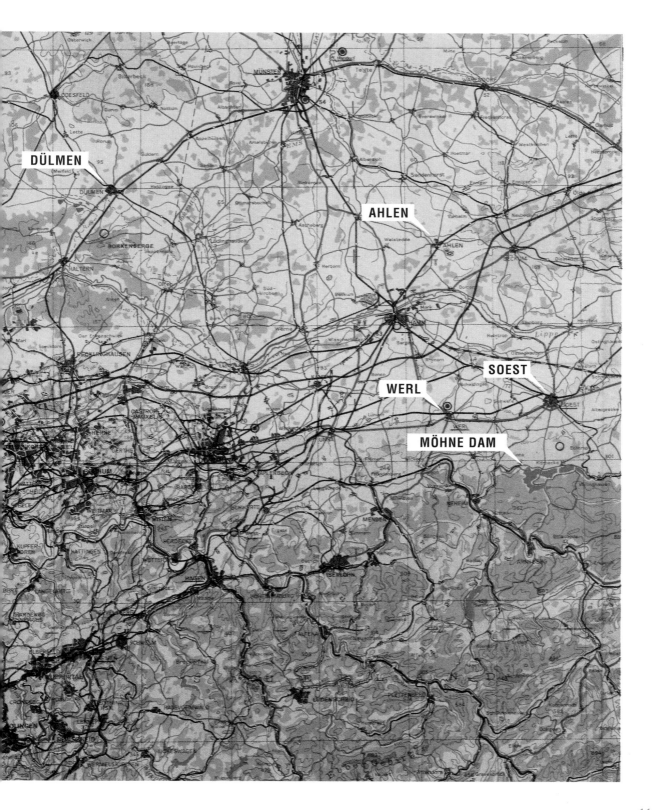

DÜLMEN

AHLEN

SOEST

WERL

MÖHNE DAM

The Möhne Dam: Hopgood of the First Wave was lost here. After the dam was breached, floodwater met the Ruhr River at Neheim-Hüsten and flowed west, causing damage at Wickede and Fröndenberg and further along the river's length.

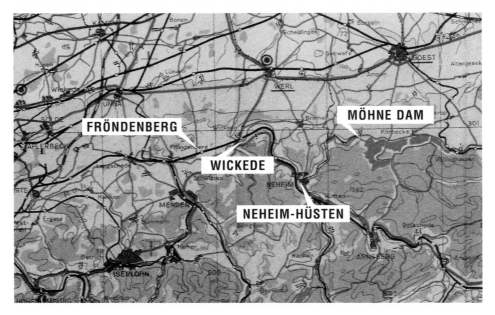

Once the disturbance on the reservoir had quietened, Gibson called in Hopgood to attack, just as Maudslay and Knight arrived: 'Cooler 2, it's your turn to attack. It's a piece of cake.' But the German gunners were ready for Hopgood. The port wing of AJ-M had been damaged on the way to the Möhne and other watching crews reported the Lancaster being struck by more flak. Gibson noticed a hit on the port outer engine, but the port inner (which supplied its power) must have been damaged too, because Burcher could not operate his rear turret. The starboard wing was also hit, and amid the confusion 'Upkeep' was dropped late, bounced over the wall and landed on the power station below. As instructed, Hopgood's wireless operator fired a red Very light as the Lancaster crossed the dam, when Simpson noted that AJ-M was already engulfed in flames – almost certainly because a petrol tank was alight. Gibson, Maltby, and Shannon's bomb-aimer Sumpter saw the aircraft struggle to about 500 feet. Then one wing fell off as it blew up and the burning remains came down near the village of Ostönnen, four miles to the north-west. In his report Gibson suggested that due to the pilot's heroic effort to gain height some of the crew might have baled out. Incredibly three did, but only two survived to be taken prisoner.

When he realised that he could not crank the turret round enough to escape in the conventional way, Burcher climbed back into the fuselage where his parachute was stacked. He had no choice but to leave via the crew door at the starboard rear of the fuselage, which was officially discouraged because the escaper might be injured by the tailplane. Burcher recognised that the situation was critical through the terse exchanges between Hopgood and his flight engineer, Sgt C. Brennan, at about the time 'Upkeep' was dropped. The last words he recalled were Hopgood's, 'For Christ's sake get out of here.' As Burcher re-entered the fuselage, he saw Minchin, the wounded wireless operator, crawling towards him. He pulled Minchin's parachute ripcord and pushed him out, but Minchin did not survive. AJ-M, despite its pilot's valiant efforts, was too low for a normal parachute jump, so Burcher opened his parachute and gathered it in his lap as he crouched in the doorway. Suddenly there was an explosion (when the wing came off) and he woke up on the ground. He then appreciated the advice not to use that door. His back was severely damaged and he could not resist capture.

The second member of Hopgood's crew to survive was F/Sgt J. W. Fraser, the Canadian bomb-aimer. He used the Dann sight, which he described as just 'a wooden box with two points on it'. As AJ-M flew steadily over the water with its Aldis lamps on, Fraser reflected that for the enemy gunners it must be 'pretty much like duck shooting'. Gibson's instruction, 'It's your turn to attack. It's a piece of cake,' soon seemed distinctly optimistic. The flak guns on the wall 'crossed up on us' with 'intense' fire, but there was 'no alternative but to fly through the middle of it'. Realising that he had missed the ideal release point, he was about to tell Hopgood to abort and circle again when the aircraft was hit. He therefore dropped 'Upkeep' late, just as the exchanges between Hopgood and Brennan alerted him to the gravity of the situation. Fire had broken out in the starboard wing, which the flight engineer could not quell. So, shortly after crossing the dam, Hopgood ordered the crew to bale out. In accordance with the escape manual, Fraser pulled open the hatch in the floor and knelt down. The trees below looked 'awful damned close', and he reckoned that he had little chance of living if he made the normal parachute exit. So, not dissimilar to Burcher, he pulled the ripcord inside the aircraft and let the canopy open in front of him and pull him out. 'The tail wheel whizzed by my ear,' before he swung into a vertical position and touched the ground in seconds. He landed uninjured, but while he was in the air he saw AJ-M crash. Behind him, the self-destructive fuze did its job. Activating ninety seconds after leaving the Lancaster, 'Upkeep' demolished the power station with its seven transformers in 'a gigantic flash'.

With the wreckage of Hopgood's aircraft burning fiercely in the distance, the enemy defences fully alert and two 'Upkeeps' dropped without success, Operation Chastise teetered on the brink of failure, but at this point Gibson's leadership and Martin's courage ensured that it did not falter. Ten minutes after Gibson, Martin began the third attack on the Möhne Dam. To distract the flak gunners Gibson flew on slightly ahead of him to starboard before crossing the dam and turning to port so that his rear gunner could engage the three 20mm guns in the meadow below. As Trevor Roper did so, Martin attacked the dam. AJ-P was hit, but the flight engineer, Whittaker, knew that none of the full tanks had suffered, and the pilot experienced no difficulty in handling the Lancaster. At 0038 Hay dropped the third 'Upkeep' at the Möhne. The pall of smoke from the burning power station and flak gun discharges prevented Simpson in the rear turret from seeing the number of bounces. Although a huge waterspout did rise, the wall held, because this 'Upkeep' had veered off track and exploded close to the left-hand (western) bank of the Möhne Reservoir. It thoroughly drenched gunners on the adjacent tower, officially bursting 'about twenty yards short'. 'Goner 58A' was sent to Grantham. The dam remained unbroken.

Gibson called up Young, the fourth aircraft. This time Gibson patrolled the air side of the dam to distract the flak gunners, adding to their confusion by switching on and off his landing lights. As he did so, and five minutes after Martin's attack, AJ-A came over the Heve spit, with Martin (who had become deputy leader at the Möhne with Hopgood's loss) flying on his left to give support. Gibson noted that Young's 'Upkeep' achieved 'three good bounces', apparently exploding in contact with the dam. Another huge spout of water went up, but the dam apparently still held. 'Goner 78A' was transmitted. Because of the delay in its collapse, nobody at this moment realised that Young had breached the Möhne Dam. Discounting Hopgood's effort, when 'Upkeep' had cleared the wall, three attacks had brought success as staff officers had predicted, though Wallis might argue that none of the first three aircraft had released the weapon in strict accordance with his instructions. Young was probably the first to do so.

Nevertheless, none of this was immediately obvious, and Gibson ordered the fifth Lancaster, AJ-J, to attack. This time he flew in on Maltby's right, with Martin on the left. Maltby later complained that with the moon behind him he was conveniently silhouetted for the gunners. But both towers were clearly visible and, after establishing the correct height, he attacked at a groundspeed of 223m.p.h. Suddenly he saw that 'the crown of the wall was already crumbling ... [with] a tremendous amount of debris on top.' There was a 'breach in the centre of the dam' – visual proof of Young's success. Maltby therefore veered slightly to port and dropped 'Upkeep' at 0049. It bounced four times, struck the dam and exploded. He reported: 'Our load sent up water and mud to a height of a thousand feet. The spout of water was silhouetted against the moon. It rose with tremendous speed and then gently fell back. You could see the shock wave at the base of the jet.' Quite why 'Goner 78A' went to Grantham at 0050 is unclear, but it was soon overtaken by events.

Once the water had fallen back, Gibson went in closer and saw water pouring through the shattered dam to surge down the valley 'like stirred porridge in the moonlight'. While agreeing that the result was 'wizard', in his log Maltby's navigator added 'flak none too light'. Telling Shannon, next in line, not to attack, at 0056 Gibson ordered his wireless operator Hutchison to transmit 'Nigger' – the signal for success. The seven surviving Lancasters circled to survey the damage. Shannon thought it 'a fabulous sight' and found it 'almost impossible to describe the elation of success'. Gibson later wrote that 'this was a tremendous sight, a sight which probably no man will ever see again'. Simpson, Martin's rear gunner, similarly recorded in later years: 'I have vivid memories of seeing a huge sheet of water as the dam gave way.'

They could not linger. This was only part of their task. In accordance with the operational plan, Martin and Maltby turned for home. Gibson, accompanied by Young (now deputy leader, as arranged) ordered the three Lancasters still with 'Upkeep' (those of Shannon, Maudslay and Knight) to set course for 'B target' (the Eder), an estimated fourteen minutes' flying time away. The aircraft would make their way individually, not in formation.

Back at Grantham, those waiting relied on the W/T transmissions for information about Operation Chastise's progress. Harris, who had been driven up from High Wycombe, admitted that there was 'a considerable state of excitement' among those present. Cochrane, Whitworth and Wallis had seen the first two waves off at Scampton before leaving at 2230 for 5 Group Headquarters. They joined Harris, Satterly and the duty staff in the operation room, where Dunn, the Chief Signals Officer, sat on a raised platform along one side of the long, narrow underground room. Satterly agreed with Harris that it was all 'very exciting', especially as Dunn could contact the crews in the air by W/T. At Scampton, Jeffree was among those who passed the time in the mess, where Summers lounged in a comfy chair and the bar had been re-opened.

In the 5 Group ops. room, while the senior officers talked quietly, Wallis paced up and down anxiously; to Cochrane he appeared to be 'having kittens'. As each W/T message came in, Dunn quickly decoded it. Transmission was so effective that Cochrane could ask him to question Gibson 'and obtain a reply in a minute'. After the first signal of 'Goner' without success, Wallis breathed aloud, 'No, it's no good.' Then came a thirteen-minute delay between Gibson's signal and Young's, for some reason received three minutes before Martin's. Young's 'Goner', apparently without success, after such a long delay made Wallis bury his face in his hands. It caused even more dismay among those who knew that Hopgood and Martin were due to attack before Young. Satterly had a mental picture of utter disaster: two Lancasters already lost. Within four minutes, however, 'Nigger' had been received and confirmed. Satterly saw Wallis jump into the air and pump both arms vigorously towards the ceiling. As others vied to shake his hand, Harris congratulated him with the admission, 'Wallis, I didn't believe a word you said, when you came to see me. But now you could sell me a pink elephant.' The scene of elation stayed vividly with Cochrane and Satterly ever after. After so many years of trying and so many failed schemes, the Möhne Dam had at last been breached.

While these celebrations continued, the five Lancasters making their way towards the Eder ran across no opposition, but due to misty conditions had considerable difficulty in locating the target. Gibson reached the reservoir too far west. Having realised his error and having begun to fly east, he spent a hair-raising five minutes negotiating the narrow, winding stretch of water lying beneath the steep tree-covered sides that contributed to the general murkiness. Fortunately, the area around the dam was clear, and Young quickly joined Gibson there. However, neither of them had an 'Upkeep'. The other three were nowhere to be seen. Like Gibson, Shannon had initially flown the wrong way up the reservoir until corrected on to an easterly course by his navigator to find what he thought was the target. Extraordinarily, a smaller dam at Rehbach, 2.5 kilometres (1½ miles) west of the Eder, was also on the eastern side of a sharp bend. Puzzled that no other aircraft was around, he was about to commence an attack when Gibson called up over the R/T. The Squadron Commander then sent up red Very lights to indicate his position, towards which Shannon flew.

After the three Lancasters with 'Upkeep' arrived, the five aircraft circled to discuss exactly how the attack should be carried out. Fortunately there were no flak defences,

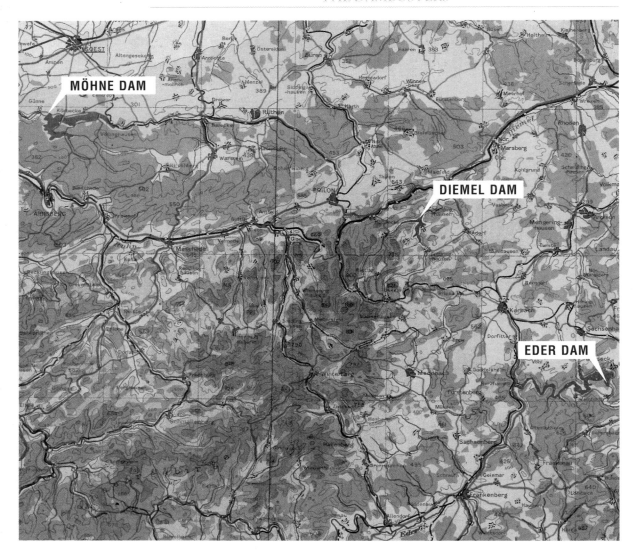

MÖHNE DAM

DIEMEL DAM

EDER DAM

The Eder Dam: after attacking the Möhne, Gibson's wave flew to the Eder, some fifty miles south-east. Following the dam's destruction, floodwater flowed east into the Fulda and Weser valleys (off the map). The Diemel Dam was a target, but would not be attacked.

though fighters remained a constant fear. Without a model to study at Scampton, photos could not convey the true nature of the terrain. Gibson decided that the only feasible method of approach, given the poor visibility in the near distance and his need visually to co-ordinate the attacks, was for each Lancaster to dive from 1000 feet, with the prominent Waldeck Castle immediately to port, towards a spot west of the spit in front of the dam, bank sharp left ('a split-arse turn', according to Shannon), hop over the spit and line up on the dam.

With the night fast ebbing, Gibson was anxious to press on with attacking the Eder. Shortly before 0130 he ordered in Shannon, but three or four times he dived over the castle, cleared the spit and flew towards the wall, only to have difficulty in getting the right height. Without releasing 'Upkeep' on any of these runs, each time he pulled up sharply over the hill beyond the dam wall with the spinning weapon still clamped in position. It was 'a bit hairy', he recalled. Maudslay then tried twice with similar results, before Shannon was called in once more. Two more aborted efforts occurred until, on the third of these runs at 0139, he dropped 'Upkeep' at 220m.p.h. groundspeed in 'bright moonlight, no cloud'. 'Upkeep' bounced twice before striking the dam, and the explosion was followed by the familiar waterspout to an estimated 1000 feet. Shannon used his landing lights to illuminate the far hill as he climbed to safety. The crew of AJ-L felt sure that they had damaged the dam and 'Goner 79B', indicating a small breach, was signalled to Grantham. The damage, though, was not decisive.

Maudslay now made his third attempt, and Gibson noted something hanging down from the Lancaster, which he believed had been hit on the way to the Möhne. Maudslay's bomb-aimer dropped 'Upkeep' late, but instead of clearing the wall like Hopgood's, it hit the parapet hard and detonated 'with a cordite flash'. Before that happened a red Very light was fired, which indicated that Maudslay's Lancaster had cleared the dam wall before 'Upkeep' exploded; Sumpter and Hobday in Knight's crew confirmed this. Gibson later wrote that 'Upkeep' exploded 'with a slow, yellow, vivid flame which lit up the whole valley like daylight for just a few seconds'. He observed that at this moment, the aircraft was 'banking steeply a few feet above', but his perspective was distorted. Even if released late, 'Upkeep' would have slowed behind Maudslay's aircraft, which lifted as soon as it dropped the weapon. So AJ-Z could not have been blown up by his 'Upkeep', and Gibson must have seen the Lancaster banking beyond the dam. There was other evidence that the Lancaster did survive at the Eder. Twice Gibson called urgently on R/T, 'Are you all right, Henry?' Maudslay 'sounded very weak' when he replied just once, 'I think so.' These exchanges were also noted by O'Brien and Hobday in Knight's Lancaster. Even more persuasively, a W/T message from AJ-Z to Grantham read 'Goner 28B': Upkeep overshot but damaged the dam. To those still circling the Eder, however, Maudslay had vanished without further trace.

With darkness rapidly disappearing, the Eder had not been broken and just one aircraft remained with 'Upkeep' – Les Knight's AJ-N. Like the other two, Knight had great difficulty in managing the correct line, height and alignment after 'diving over this great bank and down on the lake'. He made one dummy run during which O'Brien 'never thought we would get over the mountain' beyond the dam. The rear gunner recalled how meticulously Knight eventually approached at 222m.p.h. in 'perfect visibility' with the moon on the starboard beam. Sutherland admitted to being 'really uptight' because he was 'sitting there, just a passenger going down into the water and then level and then climbing up again'. He heard 'Hobday saying, "Up, up, down, down, right on, steady," and Johnny Johnson was saying "Left, left."' Sutherland, as at Reculver, was aware of 'quite a vibration' as 'Upkeep' revolved, 'and it really made a vibration when we got rid of it'.

'Upkeep' was released at 0152 and bounced three times, hitting the wall slightly right of centre. As Knight climbed to clear the hill, from approximately 500 yards away Gibson suddenly saw the dam collapse 'as if a gigantic hand had pushed a hole through cardboard'. O'Brien in Knight's rear turret also had a grandstand view. 'I was the only one of our crew to have a front centre seat at the breaching of the Eder as our aircraft was standing on its tail for the climb out… Simultaneously the dam broke and a column of water rose vertically behind us.' Unknown to O'Brien, the wireless operator Kellow was looking back through the astrodome, as he had done when Astell crashed on the way to the Möhne. He recalled: 'When we passed over the dam wall, at the Eder we had to clear a large hill directly ahead of us. After the mine ['Upkeep'] had dropped Les pulled the nose up quite steeply in order to clear the hill and in doing so I could look back and down at the dam wall. It was still intact for a short while, then as if some huge fist had been jabbed at the wall a large almost round, black hole appeared and water gushed as from a large hose.'

None of the other five crew members further forward were in a position to witness this scene. They were more concerned with survival. Johnson in the nose recalled, 'The recovery from low level as the bomb was released to clear the large hill immediately facing the dam wall was quite hair-raising and required the full attention of the pilot and engineer to lay on emergency power from the engines and a climbing attitude not approved in any flying manuals and a period of nail-biting from the rest of us, not least me, who was getting a too close view of the approaching terra firma from my position in the bomb-aimer's department.' Sutherland, too, found it 'pretty scary, as we came close to the top of the hill.' Shannon's bomb-aimer heard 'one hell of a bang' before Buckley in the rear turret yelled over the intercom, 'It's gone!'

Flying over the crumbling masonry, Shannon's crew saw water rushing down the valley, and Sumpter watched in awe as the lights of a car were swallowed by it. After circling, Knight flew back over the dam and the extent of the damage could now be seen. O'Brien thought the dark mass oozing from the broken wall resembled treacle. Sutherland marvelled at 'the unbelievable force of the water coming out and how high it was'. With excited chatter – much of it unrepeatable – in his ears, O'Brien experienced 'great joy. We felt the exquisite pleasure one feels when he has completed a difficult task perfectly.' Knowing that AJ-N had hit the dam squarely, Sutherland reflected: 'I guess Barnes Wallis was right. One bomb broke it because everything was perfect, and that's the way it was supposed to be.' Grayston knew that after the dive, they had to 'drop the machine down to 60 feet, a few seconds to level off and it was more or less release within seconds, and then climb like buggery to get out the other end.' 'I'm lucky,' he mused. 'I'd tumbled to the fact that if I shut my engines right down, she would glide down the 60 feet, which I did because I was responsible for air speed. So I chopped the engines right back, let them idle down to 60 feet and with my fingers crossed that they'd open up I slammed the throttles forward … we were spot on. After releasing the mine ['Upkeep'] we immediately went into a blistering climb.' As the aircraft turned to port, he saw 'we'd hit right in the middle, and the bottom came out initially, this blew a hole straight through it, then the top fell away, and that was it.'

At 0154 Gibson's wireless operator sent 'Dinghy', signalling that the Eder Dam had been broken, followed by AJ-N transmitting 'Goner 710B', announcing a large breach. At Grantham another outburst of ecstatic joy occurred. Harris immediately phoned Washington and quickly spoke to Portal, rather less dramatically and colourfully than the later story, which claimed that he was at first put through to a local White House pub. The CAS congratulated Harris and promised to inform Churchill of the success. Meanwhile, the remaining aircraft at the Eder faced a long return flight through defences and especially night-fighters by now keyed up to stop them. At 0210 Grantham asked Gibson how many Lancasters of the First Wave still had 'Upkeep'. He replied, 'None.'

When Gibson had led Young, Shannon, Maudslay and Knight off towards the Eder, Maltby and Martin had flown back to Scampton. Maltby took 'evasive action' near Ahlen (not the first time he needed to do so that night), otherwise AJ-J had an uneventful return trip, landing at Scampton at 0311 – the first of the attacking aircraft to do so. Humphries, the adjutant, recalled meeting him as he approached the debriefing room. 'I said, "Hello, Dave, and how did it go?" He said, "Marvellous, absolutely marvellous." He had never seen anything like it. "Water, water everywhere, wonderful, wonderful."' Martin also had a quiet flight. His rear gunner wrote: 'On the way back we saw nothing, thank goodness, but by then I think we were flying at less than 50 feet.' In his diary Simpson recorded his reaction to Hopgood's loss: 'Felt madder than Hell – returned to base OK.' For the flight engineer, too, the flight home was 'no problem'. On landing at 0319, Whittaker found that the starboard outer fuel tank had been ruptured at the Möhne, and there was damage to the starboard aileron. Although all of this was minor, in the heat of the moment Martin reacted violently. When Summers arrived at the aircraft, he complained bitterly that impertinent flak gunners had mutilated 'Popsie', his pet name for AJ-P.

Shannon arrived next, at 0406, after 6hr. 29min. in the air. He too enjoyed an unmolested return flight. Three miles short of the North Sea he had taken the Lancaster up to an unprecedented 800 feet and crossed the Helder peninsula in a fast dive at almost 300m.p.h. He admitted to being 'terribly elated' and aching to get back for the inevitable party. The total damage to AJ-L was one tiny hole inflicted by the flak gun on the right-hand tower at the Möhne.

Nine minutes after Shannon, Gibson landed, having made his way back via the Möhne, where he reported the river below the dam 'several times its normal size'. The level of water in the reservoir had already fallen considerably, with pleasure boats stranded on the exposed mud along the banks. After this, at one point his rear gunner had sighted a possible night-fighter, and Gibson had sunk low to tickle the hedges at 240m.p.h. Away to port, in the area of Hamm, the crew saw a ball of flame and hoped that the defences had shot down one of their own fighters. Fifteen minutes before the coast, Gibson called up Young but got no reply. Like Shannon, Gibson crossed the Helder peninsula in a fast dive to reach the North Sea, which seemed 'beautiful … perhaps the most wonderful thing in the world' to him at that moment. AJ-G landed at 0415, with three small holes in its tail.

Knight's Lancaster, which had breached the Eder, trailed the others, to Sutherland's relief as he remembered Gibson's words at the briefing. 'We won't have to go back tomorrow now, we've done it and we can have a day off.' The excited exchanges over the intercom faded as the prospect of having to fight their way back to Scampton sank in. Flying via the Möhne, the crew confirmed Gibson's observation of a raging river below the dam and emptying reservoir. Kellow was 'fascinated by the amount that the water had dropped.' When a single flak gun opened up, Knight took evasive action and, thereafter flying as low as possible, made his way towards the North Sea completely alone. There were a few unpleasant flak bursts near Borken, and Sutherland raked a stationary train in another small town. Before take-off he had been critical of the type of tracer chosen, and his experience here confirmed his doubts. 'I put a whole bunch in the cab; I thought, well, I'll break the boiler. But the thousand-yard tracer was just glancing off, making a beautiful sight, but it didn't do any damage.' Shortly afterwards he opened up on another train: 'Same again, didn't touch them.' Later he reflected, 'I think we should have had armour piercing, but that's only my opinion and in the minority.' Following one of the designated exit routes, AJ-N found itself off track in the area of Zutphen and Harderwijk. O'Brien then recorded a very nasty experience. 'We were flying very low during the return journey, at the Dutch coast the terrain rose under us, Les pulled up, over and down. On the sea side of this rise in the terrain and invisible to Les was a large cement block many feet high. This block passed under our tail not three feet lower. As the rear gunner, I was the only one to see it.' Fortunately for O'Brien's heart-rate, that was the last scare, and Knight landed safely at 0420.

Five of the First Wave had now got back; four were missing. The losses of Astell and Hopgood had been seen by other crews, on the way in and at the Möhne respectively. Only later did the fate of Maudslay and Young become clear. Although Maudslay had not been brought down at the Eder, his aircraft had been damaged and he must have decided to make for home at once. At 0236 AJ-Z was shot down by flak two miles east of the oil refinery centre of Emmerich on the Rhine and one mile inside the German border. All the crew were killed.

At 0258 gunners near Castricum-aan-Zee reported shooting down a Halifax over the North Sea from behind after it had crossed the Dutch coast. This time 'Dinghy' Young would not be paddling back. From the rear only the tail configuration distinguished a Lancaster from a Halifax, and experienced gunners could therefore be confused. The 'Halifax' on which German flak gunners fired in the early hours of 17 May was Young's Lancaster, and none of the crew survived. Between 25 and 27 May bodies washed up along fifteen miles of shoreline near Bergen-aan-Zee confirmed the loss of AJ-A.

Meanwhile, back at Scampton on Monday 17 May the debriefing of the crews had commenced in an atmosphere of bubbling exuberance. Sutherland explained that 'everybody was talking at once, just like a party on a Saturday night. Everybody was excited and we didn't have a chance to shoot our line. Les never shot his line anyway, so we didn't have much of a go telling all the things we did.' At 0400 Harris, Cochrane and Wallis left Grantham by car for Scampton. By the time they arrived all surviving

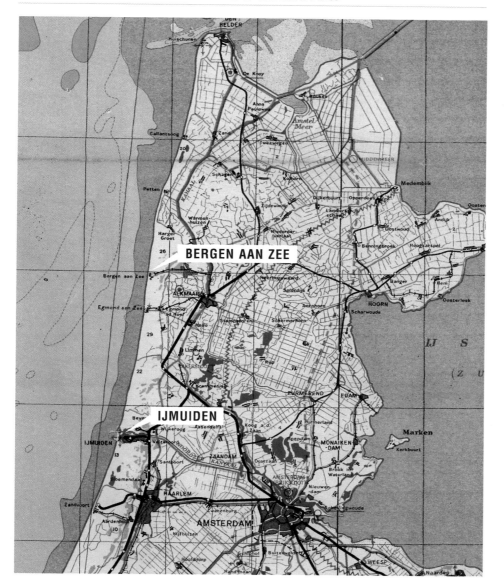

The Helder Peninsula, Netherlands: this was crossed by a number of planes on their return. Young, of the First Wave, was shot down north of Ijmuiden after crossing the North Sea coast; bodies would be washed up near Bergen aan Zee.

First Wave crews had landed, and posed photographs showed the senior officers apparently listening to them being debriefed. In addition to the usual questions from intelligence officers, each pilot had to complete a special questionnaire about visibility at the target, the number of bounces by 'Upkeep', the r.p.m. at which it was spun, details of the explosion and damage, effectiveness of the system of control, and the value of the 100 per cent tracer. A space was left for other comments. Gibson indirectly confirmed that Young had breached the Möhne, writing 'there are two holes in the dam'. He thought the method of control 'perfect' and applauded the 100 per cent tracer as 'very satisfactory against gun positions. No dazzle. Perfect for this job.'

Martin supported Gibson's approval of the control system via VHF and the 100 per cent tracer, appending a lengthy comment: 'Very good trip. Numerous searchlights and light flak positions north of the Ruhr against which gunners did wizard work. Rear gunner extinguished two searchlights. Front gunner shot up other flak posts and searchlights. Navigation and map-reading wizard. Formation commander did a great job by diverting the gun fire from target towards himself. Whole crew did their job well.' Martin made no mention of his own diversionary tactic to help Young and Maltby. Maltby, too, found the VHF control system 'perfect', the tracer 'no trouble and easier to aim'. 'Good route, flak free and easy to map read.' Of the Möhne, he added: 'In two cases a second aircraft flew alongside the one bombing and machine-gunned ground defences on north side of objective.'

Shannon enthused about the route, the effect of tracer, the VHF control, and the execution of the plan. At the Eder he believed AJ-L had 'made gap nine feet wide towards east side', the right-hand side looking towards the dam. AJ-N had widened that breach. While agreeing with the others about the use of VHF for control purposes, Knight felt that '100 per cent tracer dazzled gunner but appeared to frighten searchlights and gun crews. Opinion of gunner – ordinary night tracer would have caused greater accuracy because of reduced dazzle.' Knight concluded: 'Routeing excellent. Reports from aircraft ahead re flak found to be very useful. Attack straightforward and as predicted. It was found possible to gain 1000 feet easily after dropping the mine ['Upkeep']. Satisfied the raid was successful.' Sumpter, Shannon's bomb-aimer, would agree. In his log book he wrote: 'Op. No. 14 via Holland to the Hun. Satisfactory attack on the Eder Dam 18 miles west of Kassel. Average ht. 100 feet.' The entry in Gibson's log book read: 'Led attack on Möhne and Eder Dams. Successful.'

Gibson's crew debriefing: (left to right) Spafford, Taerum, Trevor Roper, Pulford (partly hidden), and Deering. The Intelligence Officer (seated), Harris (left) and Cochrane observe.

As dawn broke over RAF Scampton, a spontaneous party broke out in the Officers' Mess, with protesting WAAFs hauled out of bed to join in the celebrations. Sidney Hobday, Knight's navigator, would recover consciousness in an armchair at 1300 on 17 May. Humphries discovered an air of 'euphoria' in the mess: 'They were all round the piano and drinking and they sort of got hold of me, "Come on adj., have a beer", and of course I did.' Beneath the revelry, however, lurked deep concern, and relief at personal survival. Humphries 'felt bloody awful really, because I knew a lot of these [missing] chaps.' Shannon's crew hung around the debriefing room until 0700 in the hope that the missing aircraft would appear. Wallis was there, too, until persuaded to go to bed in Whitworth's house. There were no celebrations for the NCOs: the bar stayed closed in the Sergeants' Mess.

The First Wave had sensationally left the massive Möhne and Eder gravity dams in ruins. But in the process four of the nine Lancasters that had set out had been lost. They would not be the only 617 Squadron casualties that night.

The Sorpe Dam

Second Wave Attacks

Aircraft of the so-called Second Wave, which were to attack the Sorpe Dam, left Scampton in advance of Gibson's nine Lancasters. They were to take a more northerly route via the North Sea and the Frisian Island of Vlieland before flying over the Ijsselmeer (Zuider Zee) eventually to join Gibson's southern route at the scheduled turning point near Rees on the Rhine.

The Second Wave aircraft took off singly, led by Barlow at 2128. Nothing more was heard from AJ-E, and it later became known that it crashed three miles east of Rees near Haldern at 2350. Post-war reports give conflicting accounts of the Lancaster's end. A British summary claimed that it had been shot down, but different German accounts maintain that it hit high tension wires or that Barlow tried to land his crippled machine. A combination of these reasons seems likely: damaged by flak, AJ-E then hit overhead wires and, finally, its pilot tried to land the stricken aircraft. If so, Barlow's attempt to save his crew ended in double misfortune. He and all other members were killed and, because 'Upkeep' had not been released and therefore detached from the Lancaster, the self-destructive device was not fully armed. So 'Upkeep' did not explode. Once the embers had cooled, the Germans recovered Wallis's weapon intact.

Within ten days a preliminary set of sketches with explanatory text had been produced, and by the first week in July a comprehensive analysis of the Type 464 Provisioning Lancaster and 'Upkeep' were available. The Germans realised that the motor had fed off the power source for the bomb-bay doors, and that the weapon had been spun. Detailed diagrams of the calliper arms and the smallest items associated with the aircraft and 'Upkeep' down to individual nuts, the hydrostatic pistols, self-destructive device and endplates, where grouped under the heading 'British Revolving Depth Charge 3900kg'. Far less romantic than the tag 'bouncing bomb', 'revolving depth charge' is a much more accurate description of 'Upkeep'. Not appreciating that it had bounced over the water, the Germans thought that the spinning motion gave stability to the heavily laden aircraft before release of the special weapon. Cautiously, scientists began to recheck all the figures with the result that a German version, despite British fears, never became a reality.

A minute after Barlow took off, at 2129, the New Zealander Flt Lt J. L.(Les) Munro lifted AJ-W off the Scampton grass. Over England and the North Sea, the compass was checked and drift recorded as 'nil'. The aircraft crossed the East Anglian coast at 2154 and, slightly behind schedule, reached Vlieland at 2256, when preliminary arming of the self-destructive device took place. Clay, the bomb-aimer, later recalled: 'The sun had set when we reached the enemy coast but there was a little gloomy moonlight. I thought I saw someone to starboard skim the water and send up a plume of spray – it could have been Geoff Rice or Barlow or Byers.' Then things dramatically began to go wrong. Officially, AJ-W was 'damaged' by flak crossing Vlieland at 2257, though the front gunner (Sgt Bill Howarth) wrote that 'we had almost flown across the island of Texel when we were caught by light flak guns'. The operational route had deliberately avoided Texel, known to be well defended. Clay, in the nose of the Lancaster close to Howarth, gave a different explanation for the crucial sequence of events. 'Then we were over Vlieland when suddenly a flak ship opened up. None of us in the aircraft saw this vessel although we had, as was customary, been keeping a sharp look-out. We must have been a sitting target to the gunners below, a close target silhouetted against the sky.' To add confusion to the scenario, Vlieland was not after all quite so docile. Between 2257 and 2340 on 16 May, a flak detachment situated at the western end of the island reported engaging 'several Lancaster bombers'.

Quite who was responsible for firing on AJ-W did not immediately concern its crew, only the impact of the flak. Howarth summarised the situation. The Lancaster had been 'badly damaged … the intercom had been put out of action, also our VHF for communication with the other aircraft in the wave; the master unit for our compass was destroyed and … the tail turret pipes were damaged. This meant we could not speak to each other in the plane – essential for calling our height and speed and direction in case of fighter attack. We could not speak to the other planes in the wave, and were left with one rather unreliable compass, and very little defence against fighters. By the time the damage was assessed, we were well into the Zuider Zee, and our pilot Les Munro decided we had little chance of success if we went on, and decided to turn for home.'

Clay confirmed this account, while filling in more details: 'A hole was torn in the fuselage amidships, the master compass unit demolished and our intercom completely dead. Les kept on a south-easterly course for a while. Then Frank Appleby [the flight engineer] passed a short note down to me: "Intercom U/S – should we go on?"' Clay wrote, 'We'll be a menace to the rest.' He later explained: 'Had it been a high-level operation there would have been time to make up some sort of signals between bomber-aimer, flight engineer and pilot which may have worked. But on a quick-moving, low-level operation like this and with other aircraft in close proximity Les

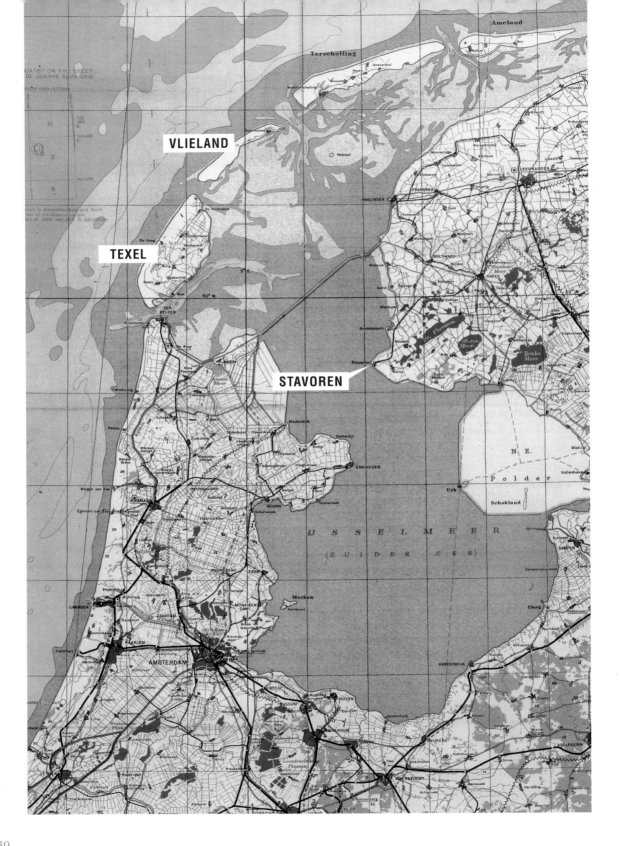

could neither give nor receive flying instructions from the navigator nor bombing instructions from the bomb-aimer.' Furthermore, the rear gunner would be totally isolated. 'A few minutes later,' Clay noted, 'we altered course for home, so ended W for William's effort in respect of this particular raid.' Years later, Munro admitted that he was 'bitterly disappointed' at having to abort the operation.

So at 2306 AJ-W began to follow a reciprocal course over Vlieland and the North Sea. Crossing the English coast at Mablethorpe, it landed at Scampton at 0036, the first aircraft to return from Operation Chastise. It still had a partly armed 'Upkeep' on board. With absolutely no means of communication, the Lancaster's crew was totally unaware that another early return was circling Scampton, and of the alarm AJ-W caused in the control tower when it came straight in as the other aircraft was about to land. Two Chastise aircraft might have cruelly collided over their home base.

Plt Off V. W. Byers, a 32-year-old Canadian, had taken off at 2130, one minute after Munro. As with Barlow, nothing more was heard from his machine, which was declared 'missing without trace'. Almost certainly this was the aircraft Clay saw skim the water to starboard, off track and heading for Texel, where it fell victim to flak. Post-war, a Dutch report clarified Byers's fate. 'During the night of 16-17 May 1943 Lancaster ED 934 K (for Kathy) was shot down by flak when it was flying on a level of 450 feet over the heavily defended isle of Texel ... and crashed into the Waddenzee.' The Germans claimed that it had fallen victim to a 10.5cm heavy flak gun on Texel. Possibly Byers suffered the same fate as Young on the way back. Aware of being off track, he may have climbed to identify landmarks (as Gibson had done further south), but like Young had been caught by flak guns firing from behind. Rice's crew reported an aircraft being caught by flak 'off Texel' while flying at 300 feet at 2257.

Aware of Rice's observation, in a post-operational summary of Operation Chastise 5 Group suggested that AJ-K did indeed fly high 'to get a coastal pinpoint' and had crossed Texel either because it was 'south of the track from base or had altered course too soon at a designated turning point'. When news filtered through that the body of the Canadian rear gunner, F/Sgt J. McDowell, had been recovered from the Waddenzee off Harlingen, the British concluded 'that the aircraft and other crew members were lost at sea'. The Germans officially credited naval flak units on Texel with shooting down Byers at 2257, the precise time noted by Rice. Whatever the reason for AJ-K's demise, the first 617 Squadron Lancaster heading for the dams had undoubtedly been lost.

The fourth aircraft in the Second Wave was not shot down, but suffered a bizarre experience. Plt Off Geoff Rice left Scampton at 2131. Over the North Sea the navigator, Fg Off R. MacFarlane, made drift calculations at intervals by dropping flame floats at which the rear gunner squinted through his reflector sight. AJ-H crossed the narrow neck of Vlieland at 2259 exactly on track yet without making an intermediate alteration in course as planned. Shortly before, as the low profile of the island came into view, 'Upkeep' had been armed and Byers's loss noted. Rice was so low that he had to pull up over the sand dunes, and once clear of the island he climbed

Opposite The Frisian Islands: AJ-K was shot down at 2257 shortly after crossing Texel. Unable to continue following separate mishaps, AJ-H and AJ-W both turned back near Stavoren at 2306.

briefly to confirm the aircraft's position before going low again to turn south-east towards the Ijsselmeer. With Gee now having failed, MacFarlane again used flame floats to check drift. The moon shining on the water made height difficult to judge, and the flight engineer was about to warn Rice that the altimeter read zero when a tremendous judder shook the aircraft. Instinctively, Rice pulled up and felt another 'violent jolt'. He later blamed himself for not using the Aldis lamps over the water. The double impact created havoc in AJ-H. Panels of the main section of the fuselage were buckled, water hit the roof inside and sprayed the navigator's charts. From the rear turret a plaintive cry came over the intercom – 'Christ, it's wet back here' – and from the flight engineer a sharper comment, 'You've lost the mine ['Upkeep']. When AJ-H had hit the water it had been torn off and the second heavy bump had been its collision with the fixed tail wheel, which had been driven though the floor to demolish the Elsan toilet just in front of the rear turret. As Rice pulled up, water poured through the open bomb-bay down the fuselage to mix with disinfectant and immerse Sgt F. Burns up to his waist in this noxious mixture. He could be excused his mild expletive. Rice had gone some way into the Ijsselmeer before the full extent of the damage was assessed. Loss of 'Upkeep' was confirmed, and Operation Chastise literally came to an abrupt end for AJ-H.

Turning back at 2306, Rice went between Vlieland and Texel ten minutes later. The defenders played flak across the gap, but Rice managed to keep below it and survive. Approaching Scampton, Sgt E. C. Smith, the flight engineer, reported that most of the fluid had been lost from the hydraulic system, so Rice decided that the undercarriage should be lowered using an air bottle, the normal emergency procedure. As this laborious task was being carried out, Rice circled Scampton for twenty minutes at 1000 feet, but he feared that with this method insufficient pressure would be available to operate the flaps fully. The wireless operator therefore signalled to ground control 'Aircraft damaged – possible no flaps' and asked for maximum landing room. All crew members except the flight engineer then adopted the emergency crash position, sitting with their backs to the main spar facing aft while Rice prepared to set the Lancaster down. As he did so, Munro went straight in below him, and Rice had to hold off. That was not the only concern. Humphries and Caple, the engineering officer, aware that AJ-W still had 'Upkeep' attached, went out to it. They found 'all the people leaving the aircraft to get away from the thing that was hanging underneath'. Caple decided that they should rush back to the mess and get Henry Watson, the armament officer, who was completely unconcerned: 'That's all right, my chaps will deal with it.'

Four of the five Second Wave aircraft ordered to attack the Sorpe had therefore failed to reach their target. Only Flt Lt Joe McCarthy, who had been due to lead the wave, remained to do the job, and he suffered a serious setback before he could even take off. As his bomb-aimer recorded, after 'a quick smoke, we got into the aircraft … and we were off or we were set for off. Then our troubles really started.' During the pre-flight checks AJ-Q, on which McCarthy 'had spent a lot of loving care … turned sour' on him. A coolant leak developed in the starboard outer engine, and it soon became obvious that the aircraft would not fly that night. The only reserve aircraft was the one flown in that afternoon from Boscombe Down by Bergel, the ferry pilot. Although AJ-T had been bombed up, there had been no time to fit a VHF radio or Aldis lamps. Furthermore, groundcrew had discovered a fault in the Gee navigational system. No spares were available. So, with much finger-crossing, the sixteen small wire-end sockets had been lined up with the male plugs and pressed together. Everybody then held their breath as the engines were started up. Fortunately, all was well.

McCarthy knew nothing of these adventures, only that he must grab AJ-T before another crew had an aircraft malfunction and forestalled him. He and his crew pitched all moveable equipment out of AJ-Q. In the process McCarthy's parachute caught on a hook and billowed over him. Having disentangled himself amid a volley of colourful complaints, the pilot commandeered a nearby truck. Into this piled the seven crew and their equipment, and off it sped. During pre-flight checks on the new aircraft, a serious deficiency was found – no compass deviation card. Once more McCarthy jumped into the truck and dashed off to the squadron offices, where Powell got him a blank card from the instrument section. With McCarthy impatient to get away, Powell thrust another parachute through the window into the pilot's lap. To secure a reading for the card, at the hard stand the compass was swung with 'Upkeep' in position, a procedure that could normally take up to an hour. In reality, two sets of figures were needed: with and without 'Upkeep', the latter for the return trip after the weapon had been released. Lack of this second set would put the crew in acute danger later that night.

At 2201, thirty-four minutes late, McCarthy at last got airborne and pushed AJ-T at 200m.p.h. in pursuit of the thirteen aircraft that he had been scheduled to lead. He did have time to note that 'in the slope of England the sun was just disappearing on the horizon'. In the bomb-aimer's compartment, Sgt George Johnson worked by the light of an amber lamp. The Canadian navigator, F/Sgt Don MacLean, had advised him that to use the roller system for his maps would be 'dangerous' should the aircraft stray far off track. Johnson therefore folded his maps, like Shannon's bomb-aimer, Sumpter.

Reaching Vlieland at 2313, McCarthy had cut the deficit to 21½ minutes. 'Very hot reception from the natives when we crossed the coastline,' he reported. 'They knew the track we were coming in on, so their guns were pretty well trained when they heard my motors. But, thank God, there were two large sand dunes right on the coast which I sank in between.' Once across the Zuider Zee and over the mainland, the enemy seemed 'baffled' by his low flying, particularly the night-fighters 'frequently' seen searching 1000 feet above. 'I don't think they expected us down there.' Meanwhile, the gunners Rodger and Batson were engaging searchlights and flak on the ground. On one occasion Rodger had a lively encounter with a gunner, both of them 'pumping away' until the Lancaster was out of range. On another, Batson got McCarthy's permission to open up on an 'innocent-looking train', which turned out to be heavily defended and gave AJ-T a torrid time.

Like other aircraft, AJ-T did not find navigation easy, especially as mist had formed in many of the valleys. Eventually, fifteen minutes after midnight, McCarthy reached the Sorpe to find visibility clear in the vicinity. And there were no defences. The crew was puzzled to be alone, though, with no evidence that any of the other four aircraft in front of them were around or had ever been there. McCarthy could not linger and the immediate problem was how to get into position to attack the dam. As the Lancaster circled over Langscheid, McCarthy exploded: 'Jeez! How do we get down there?' At length, he worked out that he must go round the church steeple of the village to line up his run. As he carried out this manoeuvre, Johnson the bomb-aimer was neither satisfied with the line nor the height. There were no Aldis lamps to help, and Wallis had warned that 'Upkeep' must not be dropped too far from the wall into deep water. The hydrostatic pistols might then work quickly before the aircraft had covered a safe distance. After Johnson had failed to release 'Upkeep', McCarthy pulled up over the far hill and circled to port for another attempt. A further eight times Johnson failed to drop the weapon, and he gathered that the mounting volume of 'rather disparaging

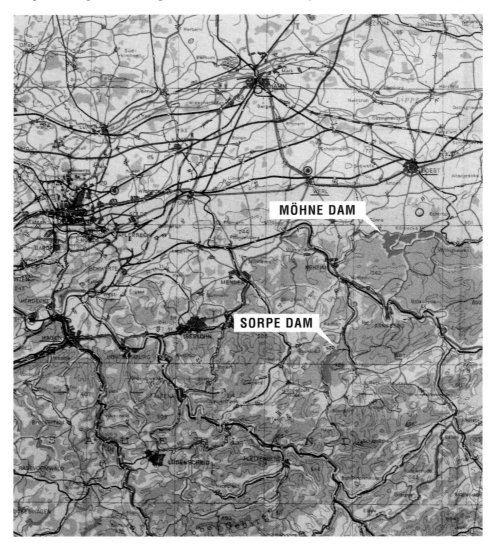

The Sorpe Dam: immediately south-west of the Möhne, the Sorpe was attacked by AJ-T from the Second Wave and AJ-F from the Mobile Reserve.

remarks' over the intercom were directed at him. At one point Rodger sharply advised him to 'get that bastard out of here'. On the tenth run Johnson did release 'Upkeep' as close to the centre of the dam as he could judge, the nacelle of the port outer engine aligned with the crest as ordered. AJ-T was then flying at a ground speed of 170m.p.h. and an estimated height of 30 feet in 'perfect visibility – no cloud – bright moonlight'. When the cylinder fell the Lancaster rose sharply and Rodger in the rear turret told McCarthy 'to get the hell down' as AJ-T was 'a sitting duck at this height' for night-fighters. While McCarthy yet again turned to port away from the dam, an enormous explosion shot 'upwards a vast clawing waterspout'. The Lancaster flew back over the dam, after the water settled, and the crew became 'really excited about the crumbling along the top'. McCarthy was so vocal that his navigator asked him firmly and pointedly to pay more attention to flying the aircraft for all their sakes. The crown had certainly been damaged over 15-20 feet. Still hoping that it would collapse, AJ-T remained in the area until shortly before 0100, when McCarthy decided that they must leave for home. 'Goner 79C', indicating explosion in contact with the Sorpe and a small breach, went to Grantham.

As the Lancaster approached the Möhne on the way back, Johnson could see only 'an inland sea' and 'no point in trying to map-read in that area'. Not long afterwards McCarthy was surprised to see a well-defended area straight ahead with a welcoming umbrella of searchlights and flak bursts already in evidence. In answer to his bellicose demand for an explanation, MacLean insisted that they were on track before accepting that the aircraft was now over Hamm, 'temporarily uncertain of position'. Crew members were becoming increasingly vocal as AJ-T pounded back and forth over the famous railway marshalling yards at 50 feet. When the flight engineer remarked upon a lull in the flak, all of which harmlessly sailed over them, a Canadian voice on the intercom observed: 'Gee, at this height they don't need flak. All they need do is to switch points.' The official report would ascribe these meanderings to 'trouble with compass', which had led MacLean's calculations astray.

Once the crew had extricated itself from this 'temporary difficulty', it tried to follow the designated exit route, but foundered around attempting to locate the lakes near Dülmen. McCarthy decided that this was pointless and ordered MacLean to back-track the outward route via the Ijsselmeer and Vlieland. In the pilot's words, they simply 'set course as route out and headed for Zuider Zee'. Just short of that stretch of water, Rodger had 'the biggest scare of the whole trip' when a flak gunner managed to get the Lancaster's range even at low level. The rear gunner thought that they were about to 'buy it', but AJ-T escaped to land safely at Scampton at 0323 – not entirely without incident. As the Lancaster touched down, the starboard wing sank and the flight engineer looked out to see that Batson's brush with the belligerent train had left the tyre flat. Johnson, the bomb-aimer, who was uncomfortably close to the ground, remarked that 'Joe controlled it [AJ-T] very well'. He also reflected on how 'exacting' the trip had been, but 'this was very much a crew effort, it was always a crew effort'.

Answering the pilot's questionnaire, McCarthy described a 'half-circular swelling of water with wall of dam as diameter' after 'Upkeep' exploded, followed by 'a spout of water about 1000 feet high'. He felt that tracer 'betrayed position of aircraft to searchlights and light flak en route', and he was therefore 'not in favour of 100 per cent tracer'. He concluded: 'Cannot say if a big breach in dam was made, but the raid seemed to be successful.'

McCarthy was over-optimistic. His had been the only Second Wave aircraft, allocated exclusively to the Sorpe, to reach its target. And, despite a painstaking effort to deliver the unspun 'Upkeep' accurately, AJ-T had not breached the dam. Four of the six target dams therefore remained intact, and only five Lancasters of the Mobile Reserve were left to complete Operation Chastise.

CHAPTER

10

Back-up Force

The Mobile Reserve

L
ike the Second Wave, the five Lancasters of the Third Wave (Mobile Reserve) took off singly to follow the southern entry route flown by Gibson via the Scheldt estuary, where they were due to arrive shortly after 0130. When these aircraft left Scampton they were still unsure of their targets, though initially they were to make for the Möhne. Once in the air, they could be sent by 5 Group via the special W/T channel to any of the six operational targets. In a sense, theirs was the most difficult task of all. The First Wave knew it was destined for the Möhne, Eder and Sorpe; the Second Wave simply the Sorpe.

The first Lancaster of the Third Wave, AJ-C, captained by Plt Off W. H. T. (Bill) Ottley, took off at 0009 on Monday 17 May. Of this aircraft, 617 Squadron's Operations Record Book noted: 'Missing, acknowledged his diversion to the Lister Dam, no further trace.' Once 5 Group knew that the Möhne and Eder dams had been destroyed, at 0230 it ordered AJ-C to attack the Lister, which had been acknowledged, but another message a minute later (and repeated at 0250) had gone unanswered. Unfortunately, the explosion near Hamm noticed by Gibson had not been that of a German fighter hit by friendly fire.

Unwittingly, several other Mobile Reserve aircrew witnessed Ottley's loss. 'About half an hour' after crossing the coast, AJ-O's pilot, F/Sgt W. C. (Bill) Townsend, saw 'a hell of a flash' to starboard, and his Australian navigator, Howard, did too: 'Ahead and to starboard searchlights broke out and an aircraft was coned at something over a hundred feet; more searchlights and lots of flak and a terrific explosion in the sky. It was one of ours; probably a little too close to Hamm, a heavily defended rail centre, and too high.' F/Sgt K. W. Brown, another Mobile Reserve pilot, reported that the aircraft 'was hit and pulled up, his tanks exploded then his bomb – the whole valley was lit up in a bright orange.' Brown estimated the position to be four or five miles north of Hamm at a height of 500 feet.

Hamm: Ottley's AJ-C was shot down at Heesen, five miles north-east of Hamm. McCarthy's AJ-T, of the Second Wave, was fired on here when flying back, having attacked the Sorpe Dam.

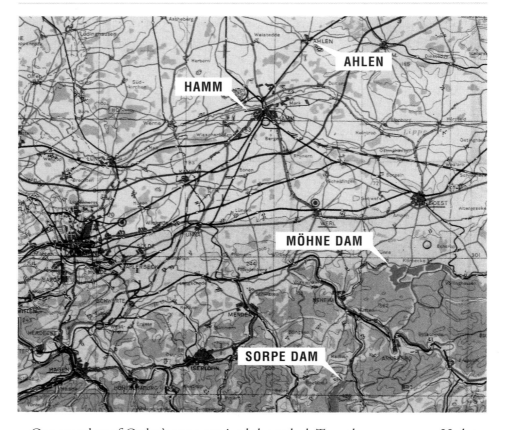

One member of Ottley's crew survived the ordeal, Tees, the rear gunner. He later described that last flight. Over the North Sea the navigator used flame floats to establish drift, and nothing unusual happened until AJ-C cleared the Scheldt estuary. Then it quickly encountered searchlights and pockets of flak, with Tees and the front gunner, Sgt H. J. Strange, 'firing away'. At one point Tees looked up to see that Ottley was flying below the height of a church steeple. About fifteen minutes short of the dam, he heard the wireless operator over the intercom, 'Möhne gone.' Almost immediately Ottley began 'We go to…' when 'a hell of a commotion' interrupted him. Suddenly the Lancaster was bathed in searchlights and hit by flak on the port side. Like Burcher in Hopgood's stricken aircraft at the Möhne, Tees soon realised, when he could not operate his turret, that the port inner engine had been severely damaged. As flames began to stream past, Tees was unable to move the turret enough to get back into the fuselage to get his parachute. In those agonising moments he consoled himself with the thought 'there's no future in baling out at nought feet with three engines on fire'. He then heard Ottley say, 'Sorry boys, we've had it,' when everything went blank. Tees regained consciousness on the ground with third-degree burns, and spent the remainder of the war in a series of prisoner-of-war camps. Miraculously he had been blown clear of the Lancaster. The remains of AJ-C hit the ground at 0235 at Heesen, five miles north-east of Hamm.

Plt Off L. J. Burpee, another Canadian, left Scampton with AJ-S two minutes after Ottley, at 0011, and was also officially posted 'missing without trace'. His end, like Ottley's, was, however, seen by other Mobile Reserve crews. Brown (pilot of AJ-F) was making a course adjustment close to Tilburg in the Netherlands at 0153, just after he had noticed flak to port, when his front gunner, Webb, reported 'a bloody great ball of fire' in that direction, and another voice on the intercom announced 'one hell of an explosion'. Oancia, the bomb-aimer, more graphically described what he saw: 'The Lancaster ahead of us flew over a German airfield and was hit by ground fire, fuel tanks exploding and the ball of flame rising slowly – stopping then dropping terminated by a huge ball of flame, as it hit the ground and the bomb exploded.'

AJ-S had strayed off track over the Luftwaffe base of Gilze-Rijen and paid the price. One Dutch eye-witness saw Burpee put on his landing lights in a vain effort to deceive the defenders. Another described the scene in more detail: 'An aircraft approaches from the west at very low altitude and tries to break through the light-flak barrage between Molenschot and Gilze-Rijen. It seems to be caught by searchlights. Then a fire spreading red light becomes visible: the aircraft is on fire and crashes at the airfield amongst the buildings and hangars. A most terrific explosion follows.' German records revealed that AJ-S crashed on the edge of Gilze-Rijen airfield (six miles south-west of Tilburg) at 0200, causing 1½ million guilders' worth of damage to the kitchens, ablutions and other buildings. 5 Group's attempts to send Burpee to the Sorpe at 0232 and 0233 went unacknowledged.

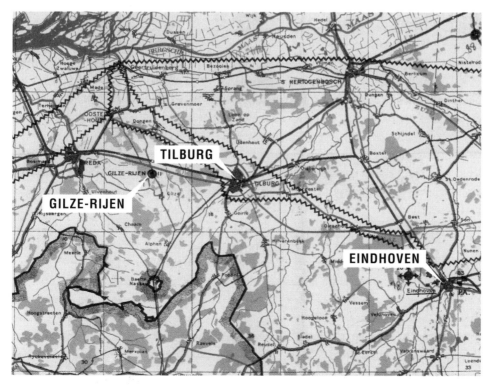

Gilze-Rijen airfield: Burpee's AJ-S was shot down here after straying north of the briefed route between Gilze-Rijen and Eindhoven.

The first two Lancasters of the Mobile Reserve had thus perished. Only three remained, with four dams to breach. The third aircraft, AJ-F, took off at 0012. Its pilot, Brown, who would soon witness the losses of Burpee and Ottley, said it was 'a damned close run thing to keep the old girl airborne' as the Lancaster struggled off the grass, and there was a stranger in the crew that night. The front gunner, Sgt Buntaine, was sick, his place taken by one of Plt Off Divall's gunners, Sgt D. Allatson. Like Johnson and Sumpter, the bomb-aimer Oancia did not use the roller system for his maps, on which he pencilled entry and exit routes. 'These maps were folded in an orderly fashion and enabled me to know at all times our ground position with respect to the proposed route. Any variations would be passed on to Dudley [Heal, the navigator] who would quickly recalculate the headings to place us back on course.' Brown and Feneron, the flight engineer, decided to split responsibility for forward vision, with Feneron taking the starboard side of the windscreen and Brown the port. Occasionally over the North Sea another Lancaster was caught briefly in the moonlight. Crossing the coast at 0130, AJ-F found itself off track, needing to make two sharp course adjustments as Heal discovered that the compass had a five-degree error. Unlike Hobday in Knight's Lancaster, Heal found Gee transmissions jammed early over the Continent. Shortly after seeing Burpee shot down, AJ-F ran into flak, and a steam train running through meadowland was raked by both gunners, which Feneron thought 'didn't do it any good'. Over Germany the Lancaster hit severe trouble. At one point Brown sank so low that his machine flew along a road below the level of bordering trees to avoid flak. At 0224 AJ-F was ordered to the Sorpe. On the way, crossing the Möhne, crew members were delighted to see a clear breach between the towers and water pouring down the valley below.

Brown's Lancaster was the second to attack the Sorpe that night, but was less lucky than McCarthy's AJ-T two hours earlier. Mist had thickened so densely that AJ-F circled for some time before the dam could be located. In Oancia's words, 'All low-lying areas were covered with a fog or mist leaving the tops of the hills exposed and thus making a determination of the exact ground location impossible.' Like McCarthy, Brown was concerned about avoiding Langscheid's church steeple and clearing the steep hill at the far end of the dam. His task, though, was made infinitely more difficult by the swirling mist. Three times AJ-F attempted to line up successfully on the crest, and each time had to abort. On the third attempt, circling to port in the murk, Brown very nearly came to grief in a valley. He remembered facing a similar situation once when trying to land at RAF Wigsley. The pilot instructed his wireless operator to drop flares at predetermined intervals so that the crew would know roughly where the aircraft was. Annoyingly, the region of the dam was now clear. At length, at 0314, in good visibility, at a ground speed of 180m.p.h. and, using the Aldis lamps, a height of 60 feet, 'Upkeep' was released. Like that of McCarthy, it rolled down the sloping bank. AJ-F had flown over the far hill and begun to turn to port when the explosion occurred. 'After what seemed like ages,' according to Oancia, a large plume of water rose in the moonlight before slowly falling back. Although, like McCarthy's crew, Brown's noted 'crumbling' along the crest, the wireless operator, Sgt H. J. Hewstone, transmitted 'Goner 78C' – 'Upkeep' exploded in contact with the dam, but no apparent breach.

It was time to go home. Flying back over the Möhne, Heal the navigator was summoned to see the floods. After one quick glance and alarmed at the lack of reference points, he quickly retreated behind his curtain to make sure the aircraft stayed on track. A German flak gunner suddenly disturbed the scene and Brown noted: 'He was not firing after our departure. Mac [F/Sgt Grant MacDonald], our tail gunner, really gave him hell.' Still worried about fighters, Feneron recalled that Brown 'got down quickly and opened up the taps'. Close to Hamm, where McCarthy had been caught, AJ-F ran into trouble. 'I had never known the Germans to put down low-level box flak as they did at Hamm. Two boxes were used, both were predicted on our track and airspeed,' the pilot wrote. But, fortunately, they 'went off ahead of us', and the Lancaster survived. Dealing easily with isolated flak guns en route to the coast, the Lancaster managed also to drop 'incendiaries on barges and other buildings we thought looked important'. A sterner test awaited AJ-F, though, before the safety of the North Sea. Crossing the Ijsselmeer before the final dash over the Helder peninsula, Oancia watched with some concern as searchlights and tracers laced the sky in front of them.

Brown put the nose down and pressed on. As he did so, searchlight beams flooded the cockpit from both sides and Heal wondered how Brown could see to fly. When flak got the range, Brown put the Lancaster even lower and piled on maximum boost. Feneron crouched down and peered up at Brown hunched over his instruments as flak shells poured through the fuselage. The gunners followed the aircraft out to sea, but Brown (unlike Young) kept low and lived. At 0533, with the sky now light, AJ-F landed at Scampton. The flight engineer was so relieved that he kissed the Lincolnshire earth. Even a cursory glimpse at the aircraft's condition confirmed that he was justified. The official report would mention a 'cannon shell hole in fuselage starboard side'. In fact, where the shell had exploded, the fuselage resembled a sieve, and the Perspex in the cockpit was perforated. It was astonishing that nobody, particularly the pilot, had been wounded.

In answering the post-operational questionnaire, Brown wrote that the 'missile dropped about 10 feet away from the dam about 2/3 of way across … semi-circular swelling of water against dam wall followed by spout of water almost 1000 feet high, crumbling of crown of dam for about distance of 300 feet.' He praised the routeing and felt that his attack had been 'successful' despite the difficulties caused by trees and hills on both sides of the reservoir. Indirectly, he supported the contention that both Young and Maltby had breached the Möhne. Feneron and Oancia had independently reported 'two large breaches close together between the two targets (towers)'. Each gap was 'about a quarter width of space between the two towers' with water 'shooting well out before falling in two powerful jets'.

Meanwhile, the fourth Mobile Reserve aircraft, piloted by Townsend, had left Scampton at 0014. His navigator, Howard, 'had visions of the bumpy [grass] take-off causing the lights under the fuselage to be shaken loose so that instead of being 60 feet above ground we would finish up 60 feet underneath it.' He never quite rid himself of the fear that they had become misaligned, even though they were tested on land and over the North Sea. Unknown to Howard, his pilot also had reservations about the take-off. Townsend was concerned that, with the Lancaster's abnormal load, the runway would not be long enough, and he felt that AJ-O actually went through the perimeter hedge while semi-stalling.

As the aircraft flew over the North Sea, the navigator noted: 'There was no wind and the moon shining on the water made a beautiful picture, one which since that night I have not regarded as a romantic or even beautiful sight.' As AJ-O crossed the Dutch coast on course in the Scheldt estuary at 0131, flak could be seen to port, but at first 'the land below was clearly seen, peaceful with no sign of war'. That would soon change. In Townsend's later words, AJ-O was in for a 'very, very nasty' flight.

Almost as soon as 5 Group had re-broadcast its warning of flak near Dülmen at 0145, the aircraft was caught by searchlights and fired on vigorously. Easily picking out the enemy gunners, Howard concluded that he would never see his native Perth again. But Townsend 'threw that heavily laden Lancaster around like a Tiger Moth and we flew out of it'. Despite these involuntary aerobatics, AJ-O found itself right on track at the next turning point, near Rees.

In his compartment, the wireless operator, F/Sgt George Chalmers, stood 'watching history from the astrodome', while he listened to information about other aircraft. At 100 feet 'incidents came and went almost before the mind could appreciate them – flat meadows sped past as we thundered over Holland and Germany.' To avoid one flak concentration Townsend actually flew down a fire-break between trees, as Chalmers recalled: 'We attracted some attention when we tried to cross a canal… We did a quick about turn. Looking out I could see tree tops and realised we were circling a forest. Some debate took place about the best method of approach and the considered opinion was, "Head down, keep low and go on through." It worked and we were safely through with ack-ack all round us.' Near the Dülmen lakes, AJ-O once more came under intense fire, but flew on unscathed to reach Ahlen and turn towards the Möhne. At 0222 5 Group signalled that AJ-O was to attack the Ennepe Dam. Twenty-five minutes later, the bomb-aimer reported a large lake below, only to be sharply rebuked by Howard: 'Nonsense, there's no lake here.' When Townsend went lower the extent of the damage at the Möhne could be clearly seen, and Howard was satisfied that his professional competence had been unjustly questioned. People could be seen clambering on roofs to escape the widening flood beneath the shattered dam. 'A great stream of water [was] rushing out of the breach and rolling down the valley.' Flying south-west towards the Ennepe over 'wooded, valley-marked country with little or no features to map read', AJ-O had considerable difficulty reaching its target. Often it deviated from Howard's dead-reckoning track to find that what appeared to be the moon shining on water was actually mist rising from a valley.

Despite its distinctive irregular shape, the Ennepe Reservoir therefore proved difficult to locate. When it was eventually found, Townsend circled cautiously. The

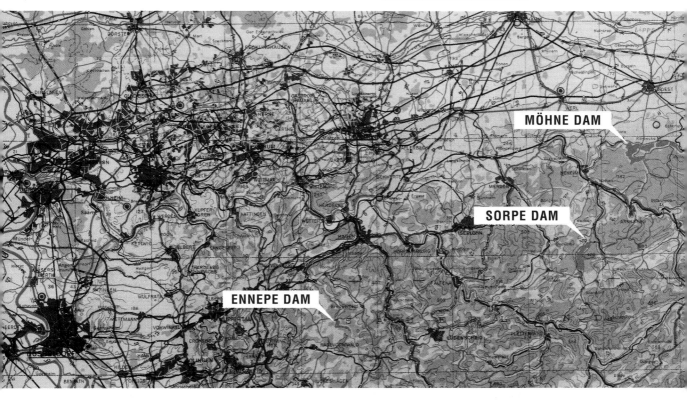

MÖHNE DAM

SORPE DAM

ENNEPE DAM

The Möhne, Sorpe and Ennepe dams: from the Mobile Reserve, flying in via the Möhne, AJ-F attacked the Sorpe, AJ-O the Ennepe.

thick mist drifting in and out of the trees gave an eerie sensation, but there was no flak. The map of the reservoir studied at the different briefings had shown an island about 300 yards from the dam, but below them the crew could only see a spit of land roughly in that position. After a conference in mid-air, it was agreed that this was the Ennepe and that the 'island' appeared only when the reservoir was brimful. One other difficulty afflicted this Lancaster: the spinning 'Upkeep' created an uncomfortable gyroscopic effect.

Not surprisingly, Townsend had trouble getting the necessary line and altitude. Three times the bomb-aimer was not satisfied, and AJ-O completed another circuit to port. Howard did not enjoy the experience: 'With the aircraft shaking horribly with six tons of bomb revolving underneath I had to lean in the blister on the starboard side and guide Bill to the correct height with the two lights.' Of the terrain he could see little, but to starboard he glimpsed the outline of a large house on the skyline, dubbed 'Lance's manor house' by other members of the crew due to the number of times he told them about it. On the fourth run conditions were right and at 0337 'Upkeep' was dropped at a groundspeed of 220m.p.h. It bounced twice. As AJ-O flew over the dam and turned to port, after about thirty seconds a huge spout spiralled from the reservoir. On closer inspection the crew saw that the circle of water had spread outwards to hit the dam. 'Upkeep' had fallen short. Almost immediately thick mist closed in, and after waiting a short while to see if it would lift or another Lancaster would appear, Townsend

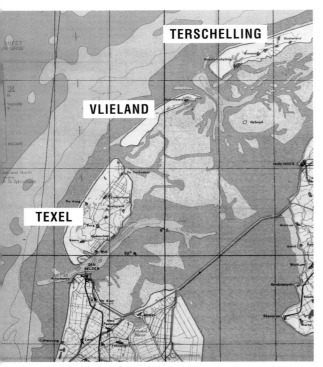

TERSCHELLING

VLIELAND

TEXEL

Last out: driven back by flak on Texel, Townsend's AJ-O sneaked safely between Vlieland and Terschelling islands.

asked Howard for a course for home. At 0411 AJ-O sent 'Goner 58E' – mine exploded 50 yards from the dam. Later an official report would conclude, 'Contact believed as ripples seen against dam'. But, unfortunately, it had not been breached.

AJ-O planned to follow one of the designated exit routes to the coast. Fortunately for the crew's peace of mind they were unaware of the Messerschmitt Be 110, which had been scrambled to intercept them and was vainly searching far above. Instead of crossing the well-defended Helder peninsula, like Rice during his premature return flight, Townsend intended to 'sneak between the islands of Texel and Vlieland'. It looked as if this ploy had succeeded until, approaching the gap, a heavy flak gun on Texel, at extreme range, began to bounce shells over the water at them. Despite what 617 Squadron had just done to the dams, Howard thought this behaviour 'hardly cricket'. Chalmers and Townsend both realised that some of the shells were going over the aircraft, and the wireless operator reflected that 'the fact that we were so low saved our bacon'. Townsend could see no healthy outcome if he held his course, so he turned quickly to starboard and flew back the way he had come before altering course to port once more. He then nipped out higher up the Frisians between the islands of Vlieland and Terschelling, and the crew could at last breathe a collective sigh of relief. Despite a faulty oil gauge, which prompted Powell to close down one engine, the rest of the flight was uneventful until AJ-O landed at Scampton at 0615 in broad daylight.

Townsend admitted to detesting grass runways, and he now had to land on three engines downwind, as eager figures poured out of all manner of buildings to watch. With oil from the front guns smearing his windscreen, and forced to peer out of the quarterlight, he bumped 'an awful number of times – it seemed like twenty-four' before the last Lancaster to survive Operation Chastise came to a halt. Utterly exhausted, Townsend saw a motley throng crowding below to greet him. In thorough irritation, he brusquely told a much-braided officer to 'wait until debriefing', when he asked how the night had gone. The C-in-C Bomber Command could not have been amused. Chalmers was more diplomatic: 'I was first out of the aircraft to be met by Air Chief Marshal Harris, Air Vice-Marshal Cochrane and Gp Capt Charles Whitworth, and at the shock of seeing them I nearly fell over in shaking their hands.' They 'congratulated me on my Morse, which was easily read by them.'

Years later, Webb, the front gunner, reflected: 'The fact is that if I had not "borrowed" an extra 1000 rounds for each gun and re-armed while flying I would have had no ammunition for the return trip. The other fact is that if it had not been for the absolutely superb flying that Bill put in, simply going lower and lower, we would not have survived. It is as simple as that. I still remember very vividly some of the power cables and pylons.' In another personal tribute, he said, 'Bill was the best pilot I ever flew with.' Of the Dams operation he mused: 'We fought our way in and we fought our way out.'

At debriefing shortly before 0700 on Monday 17 May, Townsend wrote that the Ennepe had been 'sighted by profile of hills' and that the attack had been carried out with the 'moon in half-light reflected on mist and water'. He confirmed that a 'high column of dirt and water' had been thrown up, that the circle of water after the explosion had reached the dam wall but 'with no sign of damage'. Townsend complained that 'the island in centre of lake on target map is actually joined to the spit' and 'drifting mist and dazzle from moon' had created added problems in the target area. He concluded testily: 'Considered timing too late as we were still over Germany in daylight.' He had a point, though it is doubtful whether the senior officers present appreciated this direct criticism of the Operation Order.

The fifth aircraft of the Mobile Reserve, piloted by F/Sgt C. T. Anderson, left Scampton at 0015. Its experiences would tacitly back up Townsend's complaint. Officially Anderson was 'unable to reach target, due to mist in the valleys', though the story was more complicated than that. AJ-Y successfully negotiated the North Sea to turn over the Scheldt and pick up the southern route over the Netherlands. North of the Ruhr industrial complex, however, it was forced off track by concentrated flak. Malfunction of the rear guns greatly reduced the Lancaster's ability to cope with searchlights and flak, and mist-filled valleys made identification of landmarks extremely difficult, as other Mobile Reserve navigators had discovered. 'About five minutes before Dülmen we were forced off our track by searchlights,' the pilot reported. 5 Group had first told AJ-Y to make for the Diemel, then changed the target to the Sorpe. The aircraft would go to neither. Off track, still unable satisfactorily to establish his position, with the rear turret out of action, dawn rapidly approaching and a long way from the target area, at 0310 Anderson decided to turn back with 'Upkeep' having been preliminarily armed and still on board. At 0530 he touched down at Scampton once more, the second Lancaster to return with 'Upkeep'. At debriefing the only relevant comment he could make concerned use of tracer: 'Very satisfactory – no dazzle and continuous line very helpful and apparently scaring to the enemy.'

From the five Mobile Reserve Lancasters, two had been lost, Ottley and Burpee, Brown reported bombing the Sorpe Dam, Townsend the Ennepe, and Anderson aborted the operation. Their efforts brought Operation Chastise to a close as dawn broke on 17 May. It had been a long night.

Section IV

Here We Go
Flying the Mission

'Holy Moly, crew, we are cleared in for attack – crew stand by'

Flight Lieutenant Lucy Robinson

No one imagined how much the flight Simulator would bring back the spirit of wartime flying. For the new crew, all of whom had yet to be operational aircrew in front-line RAF squadrons, it brought its own unique pressures. This was the first time they would have to prove themselves as representatives of the Royal Air Force.

At the briefings on mission day the faces of the gathered crew are very serious. They are given exactly the same information that AJ-N were given on 16 May 1943, taken from surviving documents. The only difference is that they will be using modern 1;250,000 maps over a computer-generated model of modern Europe. They decide for themselves on a different attack run: instead of flying over Waldeck Castle and making a near ninety-degree turn to the dam, they will fly on a straight heading. Why the Dambusters of 1943 chose a much more difficult attack profile remains a mystery to both historians and serving RAF aircrew.

The crew wait for the red light to start engines:

'We've got a red light, we're clear to start.'

'Start number three engine.'

'Fuel primed.'

'Turn three.'

The engines start to roar.

'Oil pressure rising.'

'Turn two.'

'Turn one.'

'OK, crew, just standing by for the green.'

The crew make their pre-take-off checks and wait, knowing that the original crew waited for one hour before their flight took off. The crew are so quiet, worried: 'My little heart's popping,' says Lucy. 'You can't really imagine, can you?' Back in the control room a vast bank of monitors scrutinises their every move overseen by Frankie, Squadron Leader Wigham and John Sweetman.

'OK, crew, we're cleared take off.'

Engine noise increases. Soon it is hard to think.

'Gear up.'

'Undercarriage up. Flaps up.'

'Passing road now.'

'Left now.'

'Stand by.'

'OK, turn left on 129.'

The new crew are airborne and heading out towards Southwold flying at 150 feet over Lincolnshire. Guy Gibson remembered the pale, moonlit landscape sixty years before that now appeared on the Simulator screens: 'Below us, and also practically beside us, at 200 miles per hour flashed past trees, fields, church spires and England.'

The journey across East Anglia continues:

'Next event passing the coast into the Wash at estimated 1020.'

'Roger, copy.'

'Nav – Bomb Aimer visual with coast.'

'Captain – Nav from Bomb Aimer – stand by for on to coastline on top now 1040.'

They cross over Southwold and check the front and rear guns over the North Sea.

Frankie gives the go-ahead.

'Holy Moly, we are cleared for take-off.'

Andy keeps in touch with the ground.

There are no landmarks at sea. The crew can ask Frankie in the control room, as commander, for Gee fixes, a crude radio positioning device whose range is limited by the curvature of the earth's surface, but that is all they have to assist them, and even then it is sometimes more hindrance than help. In 1943 the Gee receiver was with the navigator – it was simulated now by allowing the Wireless Operator to ask for fixes when in range. The co-ordinates Branty receives are slightly inaccurate and confuse him until he brings together all his other information to confirm that the Gee fix is out. The Navigator's skills have increased tenfold.

'Captain – Bomb Aimer – enemy coast ahead, enemy coast ahead.'

'New heading right on to 143 degrees.'

'Come right 148.'

'148.'

Steering around a town they encounter flak. Searchlights blind the Pilot and Bomb Aimer.

'Navigator – if there are any more towns like that please give me a heads up if we can try and avoid them by flying round,' demands Lucy.

'Yeah, will try.'

'Nav from Bomb Aimer – I'm pretty sure I can see an airfield on the nose, must come right.'

'OK, back on to 092.'

They follow the Wilhelmina Canal that leads them to the River Rhine at the town of Rees. Branty talks the crew through each stage of the navigation. As they close in they pick up other aircraft at the Möhne Lake and fly into a holding position.

AJ-N circuits in a holding position, a low dark shape over the Arnsberger Forest, while other Lancasters go in to bomb the

Molly keeps an eye out for landmarks.

Al at the guns.

Teri on guns.

Möhne Dam. For AJ-N's Fred Sutherland in the Front Gunner's position it was the scariest part of the raid sixty years ago:

'...being back just listening to people going in, and Gibson and Martin would say, well, I'll go in and go by your side and help you shoot at the flak towers, but that kind of talk was going on. I think if you'd had to go in there, that was really scary, it's tough. You might as well sign your game over.'

The new crew are re-directed to the Eder and find it bang on. Branty's skills of navigation are proving to be extremely well honed – the teamwork is all starting to work. Soon they will be called in and will see all the landmarks they'd heard about: the reservoir, the dam and the steep cliffs surrounding it, with Waldeck Castle perched on top. 'It is do-able, isn't it?' says Lucy. Tension is at boiling point, but the crew keep calm, concentrating, furrowed brows – this is a real target for them now, they have to hit.

'Holy Moly, crew, we are cleared in for attack – crew stand by.'

'Left on to 270.'

'Track is 122.'

'Understood.'

Lucy turns the Lancaster on to 122 – the compass bearing that will take them right on to the target. She has to drop down to 60 feet above the water, hop over a spit, then hit the right speed heading and height in just 2 seconds flat, an incredibly difficult piece of flying, under any conditions.

'Track is 122, adjusting for wind, maybe 125. Navs going into position. OK, crew, stand by. 120 feet – 100 feet – come left – 80 feet – steady – down a tad, down a tad – come right – come down, come down – 100 feet – wings level, wings level – come down – come left – steady, steady, good height – come left – good height – up a bit – steady – too close – good – good height

Branty checks their position.

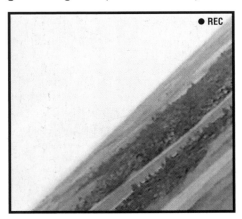

Turning in to the approach.

Lucy concentrates on the tricky approach to the dam

– pull up, pull up, pull up – full power – go round.'

Shoulders hunched with tension, face distorted in concentration, Lucy wrestles with the controls as crew members shout corrections into the intercom.

At 220 m.p.h. the speed for the first run at the dam is too slow, but everything else – height and alignment – is good.

'Profesh flying,' says Andy.

'We'll have to stay up slightly high and drop down over the ridge to keep the speed up,' replies Lucy.

The next run is too far right, then overcorrected. But the flying is good.

'OK, crew, that's good work – let's have more of the same. Let's have that approach we had on the first run and we'll be perfect,' says Lucy.

The next run is close but a slight over-correction at the end moves them too far right. 'OK, this run-in looks good, crew stand by.'

'100 feet – 120 feet – 220 now, speed's good – 100 feet – keep it coming down – 100 feet – speed's still good – 120 feet – speed good – keep it coming down – will do – come right – 100 feet – keep it coming down – nice and loud crew – keep it coming down – speed's good – keep it coming down – keep it coming down – level wings – 100 feet – keep it coming down – come right – still down – get down more – down – come right – come left – come left – 80 feet – level wings – steady – steady – good height – good height – good height…'

'Bomb's gone.'

'I think we're gonna be too late,' says Molly. The crew's hearts are in their mouths, the same true of everyone working in the control room. Everyone has to wait for the Simulator to spit out its analysis of the accuracy of the hit.

Lining up for the final run at the dam.

Molly: 'Bombs gone.'

The panel consider whether they hit or not.

A direct hit is confirmed and a delighted and exhausted crew head to the control room for a debrief.

Molly's gut instinct is correct – they are slightly off centre – but nevertheless on target. And this is exactly what Les Knight's AJ-N crew achieved in 1943, when they successfully breached the dam.

A few weeks later Fred Sutherland watched a video of the mission at his home in the Canadian Rocky Mountains. The simulation, he said, captured his own personal experience in the front turret with a grandstand view of a rapidly moving horizon surrounded by the scream of four overworked engines.

The experiment had been a huge success. The objective had been to re-create the skills of the AJ-N crew. And tough as it had been, when they walked away from the Simulator for the last time, an exhausted and exhilarated crew felt high on the intensity of the teamwork that had been so crucial to the mission, and humbled as thoughts of their predecessors engulfed them.

Reflecting on the experience months later, having returned to training, Branty wrote:

It's difficult to imagine – in fact it's impossible to imagine how it must have been for the original crews. The bombing crews especially: vulnerable in relatively unmanoeuvrable aircraft, not really in charge of their own destiny. The rate of attrition was staggering, something we would be unlikely to see again, barring the unthinkable. We obviously owe everything to the men and women who fought in both World Wars and I'm sure it is a sad fact that, as the survivors of both grow fewer, time shields us from the horrors and sacrifices made to safeguard our freedom. One cannot underestimate the extra pressures that these bomber crews were under.

Elation

National and International Reaction

'Well done Scampton. A magnificent night's work,' signalled the C-in-C of RAF Coastal Command, and soon more messages of congratulation would pour in. LAC Arthur Drury, who had worked on the balancing of 'Upkeep', heard the news over the station Tannoy on the morning of 17 May: 'To us at Scampton, it appeared to be the biggest thing the RAF had done.'

For 617 Squadron, it had been at an intense personal price. Excluding the three Lancasters that had returned early or aborted the operation, precisely 50 per cent of those in the remaining sixteen aircraft had not returned: 56 out of 112. As Heal (Brown's navigator) said, 'It was an awful lot.' Serving in the Officers' Mess, LACW Edna Broxholme thought it 'a very sad sight to see the empty chairs'. The reaction in the Sergeants' Mess was similar. Fortified by copious cups of coffee, the waitresses had stayed up all night, rushing out whenever returning engines were heard. Eventually they learned the full extent of the losses, and Morfydd Gronland recorded: 'We all burst into tears. We looked around at the tables we had so hopefully laid out. They looked empty and pathetic.' Once the last aircraft had taken off, there was no sleep for maintenance personnel, as they waited for their different aircraft to return. When the last was back, Victor Gill was alarmed to find that two Lancasters that he looked after (Young's and Astell's) were among the missing. Oancia (Brown's bomb-aimer) was keenly aware that thirteen fellow Canadians had not come back (unaware that Fraser had survived at the Möhne). Sharing Oancia's sense of loss, Rodger (McCarthy's rear gunner) nevertheless felt the operation had been 'a good show'.

At 0800 groundcrew met at the squadron hangar to pick up their equipment and make for the hard stands to carry out maintenance duties. They were astonished to find so few aircraft in position. 'Duke' Munro, the specialist who had fixed Gee on the Lancaster that Bergel had flown up from Boscombe Down the previous afternoon and which McCarthy had taken to the Sorpe Dam, explained: 'We finally discovered one or two in the north-east corner of the field next to the bomb dump. It was as if these aircraft had managed to land and had their motors cut as soon as they reached the perimeter track… [They] had flak holes through the fuselage of such a size that you could put your fist through them. The tractors were hitched on and these were hauled back to their hard standing.'

When Jeffree, the member of Wallis's staff who had gatecrashed the previous evening's briefing, woke up he suddenly remembered that two Lancasters had returned with the self-destructive device in 'Upkeep' partly armed. Not aware of Watson's relaxed response earlier to Caple and Humphries, he feared that incorrect handling by the armourers would obliterate Scampton. Thoroughly alarmed, he dashed off towards the aircraft. When still some way away, he saw ground staff in the process of removing 'Upkeep' and reasoned that it was now too late to affect the issue. Silently praying, he therefore withdrew slowly to enjoy a leisurely breakfast. Wallis was less calm. Cochrane found him 'quite inconsolable' and deaf to his argument that 'percentage losses' in view of the impact of the operation had been worthwhile. During the morning Wallis mingled with the aircrew and set off after lunch to visit the Air Ministry, Vickers-Armstrongs' works at Castle Bromwich and Weybridge before arriving at his Effingham house late in the evening.

Meanwhile, at Scampton that Monday morning the cameras clicked on pilots who had taken part in Operation Chastise, and the melancholy task began of contacting bereaved relatives. In the midst of the Officers' Mess party in the early hours, Gibson had told Humphries to go to bed and he would see him later. But the adjutant knew that he could not do that. Instead, he roused Powell and the orderly room staff. On Gibson's behalf they then composed fifty-six telegrams to the next of kin of missing

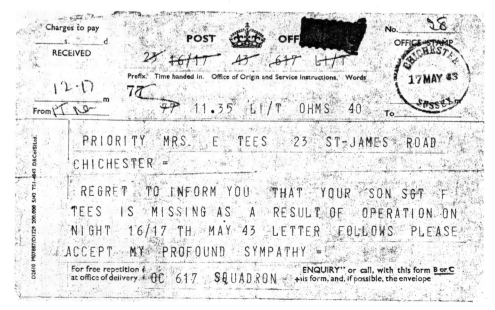

Bad news: The telegram informing Mrs Tees in Chichester that her son, Fred, had been lost on the Dams Raid.

The follow-up letter to Mrs Tees. Fifty-five other next of kin received similar communications.

Reference :-
DO/6/43

No. 617 Squadron, RAF Station,
Scampton, Lincs.

20th. May, 1943.

My Dear Mrs Tees,

It is with deep regret that I write to confirm my telegram advising you that your son, Sergeant F. Tees, is missing as a result of operations on the night of May 16/17th., 1943.

Your son was Front Gunner of an aircraft detailed to carry out an attack against the Mohne Dam. Contact with this aircraft was lost after it took off, and nothing further was heard from it.

It is possible that the crew were able to abandon the aircraft and land safely in enemy territory, in which case news will reach you direct from the International Red Cross Committee within the next six weeks. The captain of your son's aircraft, Pilot Officer Ottley, was an experienced and able pilot, and would, I am sure, do everything possible to ensure the safety of his crew.

Please accept my sincere sympathy during this anxious period of waiting.

I have arranged for your son's personal effects to be taken care of by the Committee of Adjustment Officer at this Station, and these will be forwarded to you through normal channels in due course.

If there is any way in which I can help you, please let me know.

Yours Very Sincerely,

Guy Gibson
Wing Commander,
Commanding, 617 Squadron, RAF.

Mrs. E. Tees,
23, St. James Rd.,
Chichester, Sussex.

----

aircrew. So, shortly after midday on 17 May in Chichester, Mrs Tees was among those to receive a priority wire: 'Regret to inform you that your son Sgt F. Tees is missing as a result of operation on night 16/17th May 43 letter follows please accept my profound sympathy = OC 617 Squadron.'

When Gibson arrived in Squadron headquarters at about 1000, Humphries and the staff had already started on the individual follow-up letters promised in the telegrams. Contrary to popular belief, Gibson did not write those letters. Normal casualty procedure required the adjutant to do that for him. Gibson, however, did suggest some amendments to the drafts, and he did sign the final typed versions. In the letter to Mrs Tees, some hope of survival was held out. 'It is possible that the crew were able to abandon the aircraft and land safely in enemy territory... The captain of your son's aircraft, Pilot Officer Ottley, was an experienced and able pilot, and would, I am sure, do everything possible to ensure the safety of his crew.' Ultimately Mrs Tees would learn that her son had escaped death, but she would be in a minority of three among the relatives.

In spite of the losses the overwhelming mood at Scampton on 17 May and the succeeding days was one of elation. Half an hour after Munro and the other groundcrew set out to locate the damaged Lancasters, from Grantham at 0830 Cochrane sent a message to Gibson: 'All ranks in 5 Group join me in congratulating you and all in 617 Squadron on a brilliantly conducted operation. The disaster which you have inflicted on the German war machine was a result of hard work, discipline and courage. The determination not to be beaten in the task and getting the bombs exactly on the aiming point in spite of opposition has set an example others will be proud to follow.' Later that day similar, formal communications were sent by the Secretary of State for Air, the War Cabinet, the CAS (Portal) in Washington and the former indomitable CAS (Marshal of the Royal Air Force Lord Trenchard): 'Please congratulate Gibson and all concerned from me. Wonderful work of Bomber Command is being recognised by all now.'

Wallis was by no means neglected. Cochrane wrote: ' …how much I admire the perseverance which brought you the astounding success which was achieved last night. Without your determination to ensure that a method which you knew to be technically sound was given a fair trial we should not have been able to deliver the blow which struck Germany.' Harris telegrammed: 'We in Bomber Command in particular and the United Nations as a whole owe everything to you in the first place for the outstanding success achieved.' Gibson followed: 'All my pilots and I are honoured that we had the opportunity to take part in the last great experiment which has proved all your theories.'

Among a host of communications from non-Service people came one from Sir Henry Tizard, the first man to use the term 'bouncing bomb': 'I have no hesitation in saying that yours is the finest individual technical achievement of the war.' Roy Chadwick, whose modifications to the Lancaster for this operation had been so critical, penned his appreciation: 'It was a great pleasure for me to have helped you in some small measure and I shall always remember this particular operation as an example of how the Engineers of this country have contributed substantially towards the defeat of our enemies.' To these professional tributes was added a short, moving telegram from his elder daughter Mary, who had taken part in the first marble experiments on the patio of the family home, White Hill House at Effingham: 'Hooray Wonderful Daddy'.

Wallis answered every message, acknowledging the valuable contribution of others. He thanked Chadwick profusely, underlining his pivotal work. 'To you personally, in a special degree, was given the making or breaking of this enterprise', if at 'that fateful meeting in CRD's office on the 26th Feb. you had declared the task impossible of fulfilment in the given time.' He went on: 'I can sure you that I very nearly had heart failure until you decided to join the great adventure.' The continuing stress of the aircrew casualties showed, in Wallis's letter to Cochrane: 'Will you please accept the deepest sympathy of all of us on the losses which the Squadron has sustained. You will understand, I think, the tremendous strain which I felt at having been the cause of sending these crews on so perilous a mission, and the tense moments in the Operations Room when, after four attacks, I felt that I had failed to make good, were almost more than I could bear; and for me the subsequent success was almost completely blotted out by the sense of loss of those wonderful young lives.'

These reactions were unknown to the press and the public. Within hours of the operation, reconnaissance Spitfires had brought back dramatic pictures of the broken dams and the physical destruction brought about by the floods. These were soon coupled with pre-raid pictures of the massive dams and their surrounding areas to add visual weight to 617 Squadron's achievement. Hard on the heels of the BBC's formal announcement of the operation, on Tuesday 18 May the British press gave full rein to its enthusiasm and its imagination. The *Daily Express*, describing how Gibson had flown 'up and down the dam to draw the fire of light anti-aircraft guns emplaced on it', added quite fictionally that 'guns were poking artfully concealed out of the slots in the wall.' The *Daily Mail*, in common with other newspapers, printed before and after photographs, under the banner headline: 'The Smash-Up: RAF Picture Testifies to Perfect Bombing'. It produced two sketch maps to illustrate the extent of the damage below the dams under the heading 'Devastated – By Water'. That covering the Möhne optimistically included the bulk of the Ruhr industries; the other anticipated disruption in the Weser Valley from the Eder Dam to Bremerhaven on the North Sea coast ninety miles away. Readers learned that 'two mighty walls of water were last night rolling irresistibly down the Ruhr and Eder valleys. Railway bridges, power stations, factories, whole villages and built-up areas were being swept away.' The *Daily Mail*'s air correspondent speculated: 'It is quite impossible to predict where the damage will end … the devastation done to Germany's war machine has probably only just begun.'

The provincial press underlined the rising excitement. Headlines like 'Havoc Spreads Hour by Hour' were enhanced by imaginative hope of yet more destruction: 'Third Great Dam Now Tottering. May Burst at any Moment'. Weekly magazines were not to be outdone. *The Illustrated London News* printed a double-page spread, 'A Titanic Blow at Germany: RAF Smash Europe's Mightiest Dams', accompanied by long explanatory articles and copious photographs. *Punch* produced a cartoon entitled 'The Song of the Ruhr', showing three sirens perched on rocks and armed with megaphones as floodwaters swirled around them, and a suggestion that 'any further leaflets dropped by the RAF on the Ruhr should be folded in the form of paper boats'. *Picture Post* used post-raid aerial reconnaissance photographs to explain the process of photographic interpretation to its readers.

The attention of Parliament was formally drawn to the operation. Rear-Admiral Sir Murray Sueter, a First World War aviator, declared his gratitude 'to the Secretary of State for Air [Sir Archibald Sinclair] and the Under-Secretary and the Commander-in-Chief Bomber Command for organising the great air attack that resulted in our gallant pilots breaching the Ruhr dams'. More frivolously, another MP attempted to rival Mr Punch: 'Is it true that Herr Hitler is building an ark against the flood in the Ruhr?' Sinclair gave a report to the War Cabinet of 'the outstanding operation the great attack'. His account of what happened at the Möhne makes most interesting reading. The first three aircraft 'achieved no visible result but undoubtedly loosened the masonry'. Significantly he went on: 'The fourth [Young] and fifth [Maltby] caused adjacent breaches estimated to cover 150 feet of the dam.' Sinclair was, therefore, in no doubt that Young had been the first pilot to break the Möhne Dam.

Across the Atlantic, reaction was similar. The American Joint Chiefs of Staff 'offered Sir Charles Portal congratulations on the RAF force in this operation'. *The New York Times* informed its readers, 'The RAF has secured another triumph and with unexampled daring, skill and ingenuity it has blasted two of Germany's important water dams.' Describing it as a 'most devastating single blow', the paper believed that 'all Americans will join Sir Archibald Sinclair in congratulating Wing Commander G. P. Gibson on his feat and mourn with him the loss of eight aircraft and their gallant crews.' An American radio announcer described the operation as 'one of the most daring and devastating raids of the war'. On Wednesday 19 May Winston Churchill received a standing ovation when he addressed a joint session of Congress in Washington, which was hailed by the press as 'one of the most masterly and important [speeches] of his career'. Praising the growing commitment and achievement of American airmen against Germany, he went on: 'The condition to which the great centres of German war industry, and particularly the Ruhr, are being reduced is one of unparalleled devastation. You have just read of the destruction of the great dams which feed the canals and provide the power to the enemy's munitions works. That was a gallant operation, costing eight out of the nineteen Lancaster bombers employed... Wherever their centres [of war industry] exist or are developed, they will be destroyed.' He used this as a platform to pledge British support for the United States in destroying the Japanese war industry, even after the conclusion of the war against Germany.

In Europe leaflets were dropped on occupied countries, showing before and after photos of the Möhne and Eder dams with an explanation of Operation Chastise. French readers of *Le Courier de l'Air Illustre* learned that flooding of the Ruhr Valley had been 'one of the greatest successes of the RAF' and that 'mines of more than 7000 kilos' had been dropped on dams 'which served the war industries of the Ruhr'. Breaches nearly 100 metres (325 feet) wide had been torn in both dams. 'The attack, pressed home by determined men fully aware of the dangers which faced them, has resulted in material destruction of factories, which will be further increased by the loss of water when the floods abate.' Similar information was included in another aerial leaflet, *De Vliegende Hollander*.

Wallis was invited to Scampton on Thursday 27 May for the visit to 617 Squadron of King George VI and Queen Elizabeth. Because he had been working in Scotland, he received notice of the event belatedly, but he did reach Lincolnshire in ample time. That could not be said of Plt Off Geoff Rice. Not aware of the occasion, he stayed with friends in Nottingham the previous night, and was relieved to discover that one of his crew had obtained a lunch ticket for him. He was even more relieved when Gibson brushed aside his having overstayed his leave with, 'Good job I'm in a good mood.' The crews were

APRES

LE COURRIER
DE L'AIR

Illustré

APPORTÉ PAR VOS AMIS DE LA R.A.F.

La baisse du niveau de l'eau
expose des bancs de boue.

La baisse du niveau de l'eau
expose des bancs de boue.

Barrage de
la Möhne

L'eau déferle toujours
par la brèche.

L'endroit où se trouvait
la génératrice.

Good news: a leaflet
dropped on France
showing the destruction of
the Möhne Dam. Similar
pamphlets in the
appropriate native
language were dropped on
other occupied countries.

drawn up behind their pilots, whose gleaming footwear brushed whitewash lines on the turf. Each pilot was presented to the King and Queen, although Townsend was indisposed and his navigator Howard stood in for him. Sutherland described the scene. 'We all lined up and the King and Queen came down. I think they came in their Bentley. Well, somebody told me it was, but I don't know a Bentley from a Rolls Royce. They inspected the front line. Gibson was walking with them and we were lined up as a crew, the pilot first. O'Brien and I were at the very tail end at the back, so we didn't get to meet them. But we saw them going by and they said a few words to each of the pilots.' To Grayston (Knight's flight engineer), 'We just stood in line and waited until they approached us.'

Photographers were naturally in attendance and prominent among the published photos was the giant American McCarthy with his two shoulder flashes 'Canada' and 'USA'. The King discovered that it was the Australian pilot Shannon's twenty-first birthday and urged him to mark it with a suitable party, which he duly did. That evening he could fend off observations about his copious alcoholic intake by declaring that it was 'by Royal command'. After the presentations, Gibson explained to the King with the aid of photos and a stereoscope exactly how the operation had been carried out. Later that day King George VI approved 617 Squadron's motto 'Aprés moi le déluge', with a crest of a broken dam and water pouring through.

Royal visit, RAF Scampton, 27 May 1943: Queen Elizabeth talking to American pilot Flight Lieutenant J. C. McCarthy RCAF DSO DFC, who attacked the Sorpe Dam. Note his twin shoulder flashes, 'Canada' and 'USA'.

King George VI advises Australian pilot Flight Lieutenant D. J. Shannon RAAF DSO DFC to celebrate his 21st birthday that evening in style. Group Captain Whittaker (Station Commander at Scampton) is in the centre background, with Gibson in the right foreground.

Air Vice-Marshal the Hon. R. A. Cochrane with Queen Elizabeth. Note Wallis on the extreme right.

King George VI with Gibson on his right and the Station Commander, Whittaker, to his left.

Newspapers on 28 May published detailed accounts of the Royal visit to Scampton and a list of thirty-four 617 Squadron aircrew who were to be decorated for their exploits at the dams. Gibson was awarded the VC. Of the other recipients of awards, nineteen were RAF (including the Australian Martin), seven RCAF (including the American McCarthy), one RNZAF, and seven RAAF. Apart from Gibson's VC, five received the Distinguished Service Order (DSO), four a bar to the Distinguished Flying Cross (DFC), ten the DFC, two the Conspicuous Gallantry Medal (CGM), one a bar to the Distinguished Flying Medal (DFM), and eleven the DFM. Five officers at HQ 5 Group and eight RAF Scampton personnel were commended for meritorious service.

The reasoning behind the aircrew awards was not altogether clear. All the pilots, navigators and bomb-aimers of the eight Lancasters that returned after attacking a dam were decorated. So were three wireless operators and six gunners (both gunners in Gibson's and Townsend's crews, and the rear gunners of Martin and Shannon), but only one flight engineer (Pulford in Gibson's aircraft). Grayston, flight engineer in AJ-N, which breached the Eder, and Hatton in AJ-J, which made the second breach in the Möhne, received no recognition. Only one complete crew (Gibson's) gained awards, and six of the seven men in Townsend's, the last to return. In Knight's crew the pilot received the DSO, Hobday and Johnson the DFC. Like the gunners, Kellow, the wireless operator, had nothing. Knight was embarrassed. Sutherland explained, 'He felt badly that half the crew got decorated, the other half didn't. He said you know I'm wearing this DSO for all you guys, you all did something for it. That's the way he felt, but it doesn't work like that.' Despite his personal disappointment, Sutherland thought Knight fully deserved his award and was 'proud' to be part of the organisation, whose commanding officer received the VC.

Off to the Palace: members of 617 Squadron at Grantham station on 21 June 1943, about to travel to London for the award ceremony the next day.

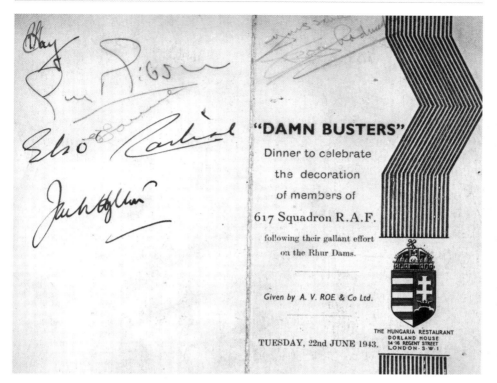

"DAMN BUSTERS"

Dinner to celebrate
the decoration
of members of
617 Squadron R.A.F.
following their gallant effort
on the Rhur Dams.

Given by A. V. ROE & Co Ltd.

TUESDAY, 22nd JUNE 1943.

THE HUNGARIA RESTAURANT
DORLAND HOUSE
14·16 REGENT STREET
LONDON·S·W·1

Opposite Above Buckingham Palace, 22 June 1943: Gibson (centre) with Maltby behind him to his right and Martin, Shannon and McCarthy to his left.

Opposite Below Gibson with Roy Chadwick, chief designer at Avro, who received his CBE at the same ceremony.

Left Celebration: a menu card for the dinner given by Avro at The Hungaria Restaurant on Regent Street. Note the punning 'Damn Busters', and the signatures of Gibson (left) and Chadwick (right).

With the exception of one aircrew member, who was sick, thirty-three of the awards were made at Buckingham Palace on the morning of 22 June by the Queen, as the King was in the Middle East. Webb quipped that it was necessary for the Queen to carry out the investiture because there was no guarantee 'this lot would still be around when the King got back'. At the ceremony Roy Chadwick was made a Commander of the British Empire for his work as an aeronautical engineer. That evening, those decorated were joined by their families and other members of the squadron, like Powell and the adjutant Humphries, and Vickers-Armstrongs and Avro staff at a dinner given by 'A. V. Roe & Co Ltd' at the Hungaria Restaurant, Lower Regent Street. Wallis brought before and after photos of the Möhne Dam, which had been previously given to him. Gibson was snapped signing in the breach and other aircrew members added their signatures along the exposed banks of the drained reservoir. Both framed pictures would thereafter proudly adorn Wallis's study, 'a historical record of this outstanding accomplishment on the part of the RAF'.

On 23 May the newspapers covered the Palace investiture in depth, with copious photos of the recipients inside and outside the gates. The *Daily Sketch* referred to the 'dam-busters' and enthused about 'a remarkable scene as Queen Elizabeth stood alone on the dais in the Throne Room'. The *Daily Mirror* quoted Gibson: 'I'm very glad to get that over, though the Queen was most charming. She told me the King regretted that he could not be there.' The *New York Times* printed a photo of the American McCarthy, who received the DSO to add to his existing DFC. Papers in New Zealand,

Romance: outside Buckingham Palace on 22 June 1943 are David Shannon and Section Officer Ann Fowler, whom he married after meeting her request to shave off his moustache.

Canada, Australia and throughout the Commonwealth had photos and accounts of the investiture, taking the opportunity once more to recount details of the attack on the dams. Catching a whiff of romance, photographers showed the Australian David Shannon, who was awarded a DSO, with Section Officer Ann Fowler, an intelligence officer at Scampton. They would soon be married, a social by-product of Operation Chastise.

AVM the Hon R. A. Cochrane declared himself 'very, very proud' to be associated with 'a brilliant idea, brilliantly carried out by Guy Gibson'. Capturing the prevailing mood, Flt Lt G. E. (Eddie) Pine, the intelligence officer who would later serve on the same station as Gibson, reflected that the news was 'marvellous, terrific … a tonic like Winston Churchill's speeches'.

Disaster

Impact on Germany

Understandably the reaction in Germany was not so joyful, particularly around the broken dams. In the village of Günne, just below the Möhne Dam, the air-raid warning went at 2330 on Sunday 16 May. William Strotkamp, a police reservist on duty at the large power station by the dam wall, warned the chief engineer, Klemens Köhler, of the alert, then sheltered in a slit trench in the nearby woods. When the attacks started, he realised that they were from the reservoir side, left the trench and clambered higher up the bank. From there he saw what happened, and when the breach occurred immediately tried to phone his headquarters in Soest.

However, the chief of police at Soest, Lieutenant-Colonel Hilse, was already on the move. On seeing enemy aircraft fly towards the dam, then flak, he was told that, although the dam was under attack, it had not been damaged. Nevertheless, Hilse decided to set out by car for the Möhne, arriving at 0108 to find it 'already damaged'. It had, in reality, been breached. The Möhne guard book entry for the night would be more explicit. 'The raid was executed by several enemy aircraft. The power station was completely destroyed, and the dam so heavily damaged between the two towers that the water poured out with a terrific force into the lower valley.'

Precisely how that happened was far from clear at the time. One eyewitness was Köhler, the power station chief engineer whom Strotkamp had warned of danger and who had also received a warning from 'the observers on the Bismarck Tower' near Soest. Köhler and other engineers at the power station had long been worried that breaching of the dam would bring a catastrophic flood and had in vain asked for the reservoir's capacity to be reduced to 80 million cubic metres. Hearing aircraft approaching from the north, Köhler feared that the dreaded attack was imminent, and immediately phoned his superiors in Niederensee and Neheim. He was told not to fuss, and later complained strongly that not only was he ignored, but also that no warning was issued lower down the valley in time for inhabitants to seek shelter.

Köhler went to the door of the building, which was situated on the edge of the compensating basin and separated from the dam wall by a 50-yard-wide herbaceous border. He watched as the Lancasters appeared from the north to fly over the dam towards the reservoir. Köhler saw the flak guns open up as the attack developed, and watched Gibson twice pass overhead pursued by shells from the six gunners on and below the dam wall. Thus far he had seen none of the action on the far side of the dam, over the reservoir. However, when the first bomb (Gibson's) exploded, like Strotkamp he fled up the bank so that he could see both towers and part of the reservoir. From there he observed Hopgood shot down, 'several bombs' launched 'into the lake in front of the wall', and two gunners blown off one of the towers, while the guns continued 'firing like mad'. Köhler 'saw the catastrophe coming' without being able to 'help my cousins and nephews' who lived close by 'nor forester Wierleuke with his thirty paying guests on holiday, nor the people at Neheim, Niederensee and Himmelpforten'. 'Down there in Neheim they had answered my warning with "Don't tell us any fairy tales,"' he added bitterly.

Another police reservist, Hannermann, lived at Körbecke, on the Möhne sleeve of the reservoir close to the bridge over which the 617 Squadron Lancasters dived to commence their approach run. There the air-raid warning did not go until 0010, when he jumped on his motorcycle and made for the dam. His summary of the sequence of attacks was utterly confused, showing just how effective the diversionary tactics of Gibson and Martin had been. But he did describe four-engine bombers crossing the water from the east at a height of 10 metres (33 feet), one 'special bomb' exploding 'just before' the double torpedo net (25 metres – 27 yards – from the dam) producing 'a 10-metre-high whirlpool'. After the power station had been hit, 'the electricity stored in the batteries was suddenly set free under a gigantic light reflex similar to lightning, which probably doubled the effect of the explosion.' 'One aircraft showed smoke' and 'landed' beyond the dam. Yet another witness, named Kleeschulte, commented on the 'very clear moonlight' and aircraft orbiting 'for a while' in the vicinity of the Möhne. Then 'one aircraft which was brightly illuminated crossed directly about the Möhne Lake several times while the anti-aircraft artillery posted on the dam was firing at it.'

The report of the officer-in-charge of the 3/840 flak contingent at the Möhne, Lt Widmann, added further details if not clarification, while indirectly confirming that the diversionary tactics were effective. 'About twelve single attacks' were carried out, though bombs were not dropped each time. Attackers kept to the right bank (the Möhne tongue) of the reservoir, and 'suddenly appeared hedgehopping over the last wood clearing in front of the dam' to press their attacks 'through the barrage and destructive fire of the anti-aircraft batteries with great determination'.

Not until September 1943 did Dr Prüss, Superintendent of Works of the Ruhr Valley Dams Association, attempt to produce a reasoned analysis of events during the night of 16–17 May. Although he still confused the sequence of attacks, from his account, coupled with the post-operational pilots' reports, a fairly clear picture does emerge. He explained that the anti-torpedo defences, approximately 25 metres in front of the dam, comprised two nets attached to one another, 6 metres (6½ yards) apart and each extending 15 metres (49 feet) below the surface. A heavy barrel was anchored in the middle of them with a pulley attached to it through which a rope ran to a cement weight to keep the nets at a constant distance from the wall whatever the water level.

Gibson's 'Upkeep' had exploded close to the nets in front of the south (left-hand) tower. Hopgood's weapon had demolished the power station, which caused power failure 'over the whole valley area'. It had also severely damaged the left-hand tower and immobilised the gun, after which gunners transferred ammunition to the other tower. Martin's 'Upkeep', Prüss claimed, exploded near the left bank of the reservoir 80-100 metres (up to 327 feet) from the dam wall, but sent such a surge of water over the southern part of the dam that at first the flak gunners thought the wall had been breached. Why this 'Upkeep' deviated from track is debatable. However, Wallis later explained to the Road Research Laboratory scientist, Dick Collins: 'The cylinder had a further *great* disadvantage in that while a slight degree of roll of the aircraft at the instant of release had no perceptible effect on the directional accuracy of the run, the result of roll on a cylinder was disastrous in that one end striking the water before the other caused the cylinder to run on the arc of a circle.'

Prüss reported that the fourth aircraft released its 'Upkeep' 'a few metres from the centre of the wall'. 'After a dull explosion which did not appear to be particularly heavy the wall between the two towers collapsed and water poured into the valley.' He described no other attacks, possibly because after this attack (Young's) the critical damage had been done.

Meanwhile, other records show chaos in the aftermath of the Möhne action. Telephone communications were interrupted at the dam, so that not until an hour after the breach were higher authorities told of the dam's destruction. Locally, though, regular and reserve military, police and paramilitary organisations had already swung into action. AJ-M's smouldering wreckage was cordoned off, and searchers quickly captured Burcher as he lay injured on the ground and Fraser as he emerged from hiding in a cornfield. Fraser was driven to nearby Werl airfield and taken into Luftwaffe custody. After interrogation and seven days in solitary confinement, as he disarmingly later revealed, the Germans 'found out where I'd come from'. He felt 'pretty damned good', though, when an officer told him that the operation had 'accomplished as much as 100 normal air-raids'.

That operation had ripped a gap 76 metres (250 feet) broad and 22 metres (72 feet) deep from the Möhne Dam between the two towers. The anti-torpedo nets were dragged through the breach and left stranded on the side of the equalising basin, while the 20-ton turbine of the power station was carried 100 metres (109 yards) downstream. Of the 132.2 million cubic metres of water in the reservoir, 116 escaped in twelve hours. In the flood, buildings up to a distance of 65 kilometres (41 miles) from the dam were destroyed, as were bridges 50 kilometres (31 miles) away. Before

many of these bridges collapsed, the water rose to 2 metres (6½ feet) above them. Within six hours floodwater had reached the junction of the Ruhr (into which the Möhne flowed) and the Rhine rivers 148.5 kilometres (93 miles) distant. There the water level remained 4 metres above normal 25½ hours after the breach.

'At about 0055,' according to German records, the tidal wave reached Neheim, 8 miles from the dam where the Möhne and Ruhr rivers met. At the narrowest point of the Möhne valley, floodwater reached a height of 50 feet. As it flowed through Neheim at an estimated 15m.p.h., it was 30 feet. Behind lay a swathe of destruction. At the Möhne the large power station (4,800kW capacity) and the smaller one on the edge of the compensating basin (300kW) had been demolished. Relatively few houses were destroyed in Günne, which lay on higher ground, though thirty people were killed. Himmelpforten-Niederensee, on lower ground 4 kilometres (2½ miles) below the dam, lost more property, but incurred only eight deaths. Despite the earlier alert, at Himmelpforten many had remained in bed, and Father Berkenkopf desperately rang the bell of the old monastery church in an urgent additional warning before the building collapsed and he lost his own life. Heavy loss of life and destruction occurred at Neheim-Hüsten, where the peril of the approaching flood was not appreciated by the authorities. Some 1200 foreign workers remained confined in air-raid shelters there and many would be drowned. The administrative authorities at Soest, responsible for the region, declared the damage in the Möhne valley 'catastrophic' and demanded one million Reichsmarks for repairs.

Opposite The Möhne Dam: note the cross-section of the dam wall, the tower used to house a flak gun, the debris on the crown, and the artificial trees for attempted camouflage.

An aerial view of damage to the Moehen Dam, showing the water pouring through the breach, the drained reservoir beyond, and the large power station beneath the wall destroyed.

The Möhne Dam: the breach after the water had stopped flowing through. Note the damage to the tower on the right.

Between Neheim and the Rhine, the Ruhr Valley also suffered. Wickede had three factories, an iron foundry and its waterworks badly damaged, and all gas and electricity supplies cut off. When no aircraft had appeared after an initial police alert, people had gone back to their houses. The only warning system was for fire, and when this sounded many thought it the all-clear and paid for the mistake with their lives. A road and a railway bridge were heavily damaged and farmland in the area strewn with uprooted trees, debris and furniture. Fröndenberg, 25 kilometres (16 miles) below the dam, was hit at 0300. Along the length of the Ruhr, pumping stations were affected and, ironically, many towns without water supplies. The power station at Herdecke (132,000kW) was flooded to a depth of 2 metres.

The final official figures for the Möhne and Ruhr valleys would show eleven factories totally destroyed, 114 damaged, twenty-five road or rail bridges destroyed, and twenty-one railway bridges damaged, apart from numerous power stations, pumping stations, and water and gas supply facilities also affected. In human terms, below the Möhne there were 1294 casualties: 476 German dead with 69 missing, and 593 foreigners dead, 156 missing.

The picture at the Eder was at once both similar and different, particularly as the aim was primarily to disrupt river and canal communications rather than to destroy industrial capacity. When people near the dam heard aircraft approaching shortly after

0100 on 17 May they were not unduly worried. Previous air-raid warnings had brought no direct danger, and enemy machines often used the glistening water of the reservoir as a navigational aid. Karl Albrecht, chief engineer of the two power stations (Hemfurth I and II) nestling below the extremities of the wall on the air side, was not therefore perturbed as several aircraft (the dummy runs of the three Lancasters) flew over him that morning. He was startled by the dull explosion caused by Shannon's mine, and totally confused by the impact of Maudslay's. As masonry and water poured through the roof of Hemfurth II, he belatedly fled up the steps to the crest of the dam to see the breach made by Knight, which visibly widened as the torrent rushed through.

August Rubsam, a dams' authority official, was flung several yards by the final explosion. On regaining his composure, he realised that he must inform head office at Hannover-Münden, only to discover that all telegraph and telephone links in the area had been severed. Fortunately, somebody else had been able to telephone a warning to surrounding villages. The postmaster at Bad Wildungen, 7 kilometres (4 miles) south-

The upper part of the Möhne reservoir almost drained on the morning after the attack.

Fröndenberg in the Ruhr Valley, twenty miles from the Möhne Dam, showing a submerged road and an electricity works, railway bridge, railway carriages and sidings all damaged.

Opposite Above The Eder Dam, showing the breach made by Knight's Lancaster, with Waldeck Castle in the background. Note the damage to the parapet and roadway caused by Maudslay's 'Upkeep'.

Opposite Below An aerial view of the damage. Note the spit of land across which the Lancasters attacked, and the hill beyond the dam that they had to clear.

east of the Eder, was standing in his yard listening to unopposed aircraft circling without appreciating that the dam was under attack. Then, he recalled, 'I saw a high spiteful-green flame rise up and shortly afterwards an explosion, followed by a din like the distant, muffled sound of a railway engine.' At that moment the phone rang, and he ran to answer it. 'Edersee here, the dam wall is broken, I…,' and the line went dead. Reacting quickly, he began to ring villages in the valley – Affoldern, closest to the dam, and others as far away as Fritzlar. Arguably, his prompt action saved many lives.

A V-shaped breach 70 metres (230 feet) wide and 22 metres (72 feet) deep had been made at the Eder Dam, and 30,000 tons of masonry lanced from the structure. Of the 202.4 million cubic metres of water in the reservoir, 154.4 million escaped. German reports referred to 'cracks and loosened spots' with 'horizontal fissures' well beyond the central breach. Shannon's 'Upkeep' had exploded in the area of the steps at the right-hand end of the dam and cracked the wall. Maudslay demolished the ashlar parapets, part of the roadway and pavement on the crown. So all three 'Upkeeps' released there had not only hit, but had also damaged the Eder Dam.

The two Hemfurth power stations in the shadow of the dam were put out of action, and two more close by. Buildings were affected in many of the villages in the Eder, Fulda and Weser valleys, which the Eder reservoir fed. Fritzlar military airfield (15 kilometres – 9 miles – away) was partially flooded, and railway and road bridges for a

Another aerial view showing the effects of the flooding below the Eder Dam.

considerable distance beyond either swept away or damaged. The bed of the Eder River up to its junction with the Fulda was 'devastated'. Because the sides of the rivers were less steep and the flood therefore spread wider than at the Möhne, a slower rate of flow meant that not until the afternoon of 17 May were parts of Kassel (60 kilometres – 37 miles – distant) inundated with 2 metres of water. The following morning (18 May) supplies had to be ferried by rowing boat to houses at Karlshafen (139 kilometres – 87 miles – from the Eder). Ultimately 30,000 cubic metres of earth were dredged from the Fulda River and 5000 from the Weser to restore navigable channels, while 5.5 kilometres (3½ miles) of the banks of the Fulda had to be rebuilt. The top soil from 50 hectares of valuable agricultural land was washed away, and fertile fields strewn with shingle and scree to a depth of 2 metres. Officially, 'millions of Reichsmarks' of damage had been done. Due to the more adequate warning, and the slower rate and lower height of the flood, only forty-seven people died below the Eder.

Opposite Kassel: the swollen River Fulda, thirty miles below the Eder Dam, on 18 May.

The impact of the damage to and below the Möhne and Eder dams was not simply local. News of the attacks brought rapid reaction in Berlin. Albert Speer, the Minister for Armament and War Production, was summoned from his bed to learn that the Möhne had been 'shattered', its reservoir 'emptied' and 'three other dams' had been attacked. Shortly after dawn on 17 May he flew over the affected areas in a light aircraft. Surveying the scenes of ruin, Speer had no doubt that the bombers had 'tried to strike at our whole armaments industry'. He immediately demanded that additional flak guns, balloons and searchlights be positioned as a matter of priority not only around the dams already attacked, but others considered vulnerable.

For two days Speer carried out extensive inspections, concluding that the scale of destruction had 'imperilled' the water supply and threatened to bring industry 'to a standstill'. With Hitler's approval he ordered 7000 specialists into the Ruhr area at once, with a further 20,000 workers (including many diverted from building the Atlantic Wall) as soon as possible.

During his tour Speer calculated that the attacks at the Sorpe had come 'within inches' of success. In his later comprehensive summary, Dr Prüss noted that two craters had been made 30 metres (98 feet) apart, 3 metres (10 feet) below the water level, and that the explosions had sent water 150-200 metres (up to 650 feet) into the air. The downward effect of the explosions had been 'damped by the material of the rubble dam'. Although the dam essentially 'remained undamaged', the concrete central wall had been stripped 'to a depth of several metres' on the water side. Another German estimate made the two craters 12 metres (39 feet) deep, a third thought them 8 metres (26 feet) wide by 4.5 metres (15 feet) deep. Despite British hopes that seepage would gradually cause collapse of the dam, this was the extent of the damage. None at all was discovered at the Ennepe Dam.

German military authorities sought to play down the effects of Operation Chastise (describing 'weak British flying formations' being driven off) and publicity outside the affected areas was forbidden. But civilian authorities in Halle-Merseburg and Mark Brandenburg none the less reported 'general consternation' at their enemy's ability to find and destroy the dams. At Kurhessen the lack of sufficient flak defences attracted special criticism, with calls for punishment of those responsible. Hitler was similarly furious. According to Speer, the raid, to which he referred as 'this disaster in the west', made 'a deep impression' on him. Hitler raged at Göring for allowing these few 'crates' to get through the Luftwaffe defences and, in particular, threaten the industrial Ruhr. His ebbing confidence in the Luftwaffe, which had failed to live up to its commander's boast fully to protect the homeland, bring triumph in the Battle of Britain and supply the beleaguered German Sixth Army at Stalingrad, which had been forced to surrender three months earlier, had been further eroded. It helped reinforce his belief that no German aircraft should be purely defensive. All must have an offensive capability, which meant the ability to carry bombs – even fighters – and this applied even to the developing jet aircraft, the Messerschmitt Me-262. Without Hitler's interference in this way, and produced in large numbers purely as a fighter,

SORPE DAM
(After attack)
K 1559
Neg. No. 24689

the Me-262 might well have seriously embarrassed allied bomber fleets in the closing months of the war.

The effect of Operation Chastise would reverberate around military, civilian and political circles in the Reich for a long time to come. Its influence extended far beyond the trails of physical destruction at and below the breached dams.

The Sorpe Dam: a reconnaissance Spitfire reveals the damage to the crown, and water spilling over the top, but no breach.

13

Conclusion

Reflection, Significance and Postscript

Writing five days after the event, Barnes Wallis declared: 'I feel that a blow has been struck at Germany from which she cannot recover for several years.' An Australian assessment agreed: 'All that had been anticipated came to pass. A tremendous blow had been struck at the German industry.'

Post-war commentators have sharply disagreed. 'The truth about the Dams Raid is that it was a conjuring trick, virtually devoid of military significance' ... 'The story of the raid is one of sloppy planning, narrow-minded enthusiasm and misdirected courage' ... 'The dams raid had scant effect on German war production; the influence of the ricochet bomb on the imponderable sum of war was negligible.' These have been among a series of condemnations advanced by journalists and academics, dismissed by Cochrane as 'disgraceful'. Many critics have pointed to the swift restoration of essential supplies and, critically, repair of the dams. The long-term physical impact of the raid had been marginal, therefore the contemporary celebration and continuing commemoration of the operation are, at best, misplaced.

The fiftieth anniversary of the Dambusters Raid witnessed a rash of new censures, including the apparent failure of the Air Staff to recognise the importance of the Sorpe Dam (actually acknowledged in 1937) and negligence in not interfering with the rebuilding process (ignoring the greater strength of the dams' defences after 17 May and the RAF's inability accurately to hit such specific targets without Wallis's unique weapon). Spice to this particular debate in 1992 was added by a surviving pilot, Ken Brown, who publicly declared that he felt the raid was not worthwhile, and that the loss of eight crews unjustified. That intensely personal reaction to the loss of, in his words, 'so many friends' has been married to Wallis's similar despair on the morning after the operation and refusal thereafter to discuss the 'loss of so many brave lives'. AVM the Hon R. A. Cochrane, however, has pointed to the achievement of such a small force. The losses, though regrettable, must be weighed against much higher casualties suffered on many less successful operations. ACM Sir Arthur Harris argued that 'specialist operations of this nature' were bound to incur heavy loss. More specifically, as mentioned earlier one of F/Sgt Fraser's captors told him that this operation had 'accomplished as much as 100 normal air-raids'. That, he admitted, made him feel 'pretty damned good'.

Nevertheless, bearing in mind that the gaps in both breached dams had been filled by October, and no decisive damage had been done to the Sorpe nor any of the other three target dams, was the operation really worthwhile?

Judgement should not be made on the basis of exaggerated press claims in the immediate aftermath of the operation. The newspapers might suggest that the 'Third Great Dam' was to topple, but the Air Ministry never fell into that trap. Of the Sorpe on 26 May, the Ministry's Director of Bomber Operations informed Wallis: 'It appears from the evidence … that no seepage was set up as a result of the attack.' Moreover, it is clear that most of the unrealistic published claims were prompted by extravagant and unsubstantiated reports from news agencies in neutral countries whose dubious sources went unchallenged in the contemporary thirst for information. On 18 May, scarcely twenty-four hours after the raid, *The New York Times* quoted 'a telegram from Berne' reporting public dismay at the attack in Germany and civil unrest due to the destruction. Morocco Radio was more specific: rioting had occurred in Duisburg and Dortmund. This bulletin went on to assert that 'the number of dead and homeless is growing each hour'. As a result, some newspapers would speculate that the number dead might exceed 4000. Bernard Valery, Reuter's special correspondent in Stockholm, estimated that 'at least six months' would be required to repair damage. And another Reuter's special correspondent in Zurich, Reginald Langford, optimistically declared that the morale of people in Kassel was so low that 'their only desire is that the war should end, whatever the results'. Swedish newspapers embellished the story of the 'Niagara bomb' with lurid accounts of travel in Dortmund being possible only by flat-bottomed boats and serious explosions there because water had invaded blast furnaces. These fantasies, although easily disproved later, have left a residue of disappointment that their alleged results were not achieved.

There is no doubt that, like the repair of the walls, much of the damage was made good, and inescapably floods do in time recede. Nowhere could remain under water for long. Yet the effect in the Ruhr was not all short-term. For example, the waterworks at Fröndenberg and Echthausen (important for regional coalfields) were totally out of action for four months. Several waterworks supplying Neheim-Hüsten, Soest and Herdecke were severely damaged and only a 'tolerable' level eventually restored. Moreover, for security reasons in case of another attack, the water level in the Möhne, Eder and Sorpe reservoirs was reduced, thus affecting future supplies. Speer may have dismissed the deaths of 'a few hundred cows' as 'unimportant', but their loss and that of agricultural products did have serious implications. Below both the Möhne and Eder dams, much of the flooded land could not be tilled for years afterwards. In June

617 Squadron: a group photo taken after the Dams Raid. Gibson (centre) is flanked by Martin (right) and Maltby (left).

1943 meat rations for 'normal customers' were reduced, the second time in two months. Poor potato crops in 1943-44 and a shortage of feed for the draught animals on which many German farmers still relied did not improve matters. In this context, the loss of agricultural land and cattle as a result of Operation Chastise was not actually 'unimportant', as Speer claimed, at a time when he admitted that the German Government was 'concerned' about civilian ration supplies.

The defensive measures ordered in the wake of the Dambusters Raid had an important knock-on effect. At the Eder, for instance, light (20mm and 37mm) and heavy (88mm) flak guns, rocket-carrying vehicles, searchlights and smoke-screen apparatus were deployed. Regular and reserve troops were brought up to cope with paratrooper landings or other sabotage attempts. These and similar precautions taken at other important dams, including the Möhne, involved the estimated equivalent of a division of soldiers and equipment (notably flak guns), which could have been used either in the front line or to combat increasingly heavy bomber raids on German towns. This was by no means a negligible effect of Operation Chastise.

Churchill's use of the Dams Raid to underline the importance of air attacks on Germany's industrial base in his speech to Congress on 19 May was timely and its

political message significant. He had recently been warned of American doubts about concentrating the US war effort on Germany, rather than Japan. The official response to his words, although not in itself decisive, undoubtedly helped to reduce criticism of the European commitment. From Moscow the British military mission reported that the Soviets were 'showing great interest in this operation and are possibly contemplating something similar'. They therefore wanted full details of both the operation and the weapon used. When this was agreed in August, the Air Ministry advised the mission that 'you should make greatest possible capital out of our handing over this important and highly secret information'. It would show the Soviets that the British were willing to co-operate 'in aircraft matters'. If only to a marginal extent in the broader picture, the operation therefore had an impact on Allied international relations.

The ability to locate and attack four dams, none of them easily found, and to destroy two of them, in the words of Martin's flight engineer, Whittaker, represented 'a milestone in the standard it set'. Hans Rump, the German Inspector-General of Fire Prevention in the region, called it a 'most impressive success … precision bombing of a high order'. 617 Squadron had achieved an accuracy only dreamed of pre-war, which formed the original basis for attacking the dams in 1937 but had proved unattainable once hostilities commenced. This professional achievement should not be underestimated. Cochrane used the example of 617 Squadron's dedicated training (2288 practice bombs dropped in six weeks) and achievement at the dams to urge greater accuracy on all bomber crews: 'Unfortunately a number of bombs are still falling two, three and five miles from the aiming point, and this is delaying victory.' At the Air Ministry, Bufton believed that because this operation showed that Ruhr targets could be hit with such pinpoint accuracy, it proved that the RAF had 'established a bridge-head over Europe'. Harris considered Operation Chastise as a valuable contribution to what he called The Battle of the Ruhr. For Wallis it had a different importance. Replying to Chadwick's letter of congratulation, he wrote: 'I do agree it is the engineers of this country who are going to win the war.'

That Knight's Lancaster breached the Eder is indisputable. Evidence at the time quite clearly showed that Young did so also at the Möhne, but the two men who in later years could have proved this (Young himself and Maltby, the following pilot who reported AJ-A's success at debriefing) did not survive the war.

Fate or luck played a decisive part in this operation. If Young had not been designated deputy leader, he would have flown straight home from the Möhne with Maltby and Martin, instead of following Gibson to the Eder. Possibly, then, his aircraft would not have been lost. In fact, both flight commanders (Young and Maudslay) were shot down on the way back. In Ottley's AJ-C, lost near Hamm, the two gunners changed position, something not shown in official records. So Tees (although badly burned) lived, and Strange did not. Astell and Ottley seem to have made only minor navigational errors at planned turning points, and Burpee to have strayed slightly off track with fatal consequences. Several others, including Gibson, had navigational problems on more than one occasion and survived.

The crash of Barlow's AJ-E especially illustrates the role of fate. Because the self-destructive device did not work, the Germans removed 'Upkeep' intact and by the first week of July had produced a lengthy written and diagrammatic analysis of it. So, in his September report, Dr Prüss could write: 'The nature of the bombs had already been established from an aircraft which crashed on the lower Rhine on the way in.' British intelligence soon knew of the discovery and elaborate measures were discussed to protect British dams in case the Germans turned 'Upkeep' on them. The 'five Sheffield lakes', for example, were together allocated twenty-eight 40mm anti-aircraft guns and forty-two searchlights.

The skill and determination of the aircrew has rightly been praised, but the contribution of personnel on the ground should not be overlooked. As Plt Off B. T. Foxlee (Martin's front gunner) put it: 'Don't forget the "penguins", who made the whole operation successful – the ground staff from ACH/GDs to Station Commander, and especially Rolls Royce – our Merlin engines never missed a beat.' Humphries thought 'the flight mechanics and the armourers, who had to load this special bomb on to the aeroplane, were the unsung heroes in this particular case.' Nor should the support of families and friends, the anguish of those who lost loved ones, be overlooked.

Webb, Townsend's front gunner, later reflected: 'If we did nothing else, we gave people in this country a lift.' Benjamin Lockspeiser, architect of the airborne lighting system for judging the aircraft's height over the reservoirs, similarly emphasised the 'tremendous psychological effect' of the operation. Leonard Cheshire, station commander at Marston Moor and a future recipient of the VC with 617 Squadron, and Douglas Bader, confined in a German prisoner of war camp, independently confirmed that news of the Dambusters Raid 'certainly' lifted their spirits. The operation, therefore, raised morale immeasurably in Allied countries and among occupied territories on the European mainland. Conversely, Speer acknowledged that it adversely affected Nazi ministers from Hitler downwards, and regional gauleiters drew attention to public dismay in their areas.

At the time, and this is the crucial consideration, Operation Chastise had a major impact on Allies and enemy alike far beyond the physical destruction of the dams. The response of the American pilot Joe McCarthy to a latter-day inquisitor is therefore apt: 'Hey, you weren't there.'

Wallis despaired that 'Upkeep' was allowed just 'one wonderful feat'. When he went to Harris with a suggestion that it be used against vulnerable Italian dams, claiming with a touch of pre-war naivety that this would force Italy out of the war, the C-in-C Bomber Command proved 'frightfully pompous' in turning him down. So much for pink elephants. Attempts were, however, made to modify 'Upkeep' for forward spin so that it could be used on land targets, but these proved unsatisfactory.

Only seven of the eleven pilots who returned from the dams survived the war. Neither Gibson nor any of his crew did so. Four (Spafford, Deering, Taerum and Hutchison) were shot down in Sqn Ldr George Holden's aircraft on the way to attack

The crew of Lancaster AJ-N, who breached the Eder Dam, with Les Knight, the pilot, in the centre.

the Dortmund-Ems Canal on 15 September 1943. Pulford and Trevor Roper were later lost with other squadrons. Gibson himself, after a spell of ground duty, crashed in September 1944 in a Mosquito coming back from a raid on Rheydt, near Mönchen Gladbach, where he had repeated his dams role by directing the attacks as master bomber. His obituary in the St Edward's School magazine in Oxford revealed a surprising facet of his personality, a deep interest in the cinema organ 'of the working of which over-luscious instrument he spake as an authority'. Gibson's premature death at the age of 25 has fuelled a debate between those who maintain that his qualities fitted him eventually to become CAS, and others who doubted his ability to cope with the political and administrative acumen required in that post. Was Gibson essentially a 'warrior', as Harris acknowledged, more adept at flying an aeroplane than a Whitehall desk?

The night before Holden's loss, the squadron had been recalled en route to the Dortmund-Ems due to bad weather. The wing of Maltby's Lancaster clipped the North Sea off Cromer as it turned back at low level, and the aircraft sank. Shannon hopefully circled, but no survivors appeared. Maltby was due to be his best man that weekend, and Gp Capt Whitworth stood in for him. Anderson failed to return from an operation with another squadron, and Knight gave his life to save other members of his crew on the Dortmund-Ems raid in September 1943. Two engines were fatally damaged after hitting trees at low level and, despite strenuous efforts by everybody on board to keep the Lancaster aloft, it became clear that they were fighting a losing battle. Knight, therefore, ordered his crew to bale out as he struggled to retain sufficient height. His last words to Grayston, his flight engineer, were 'God bless'. Soon afterwards the Lancaster crashed, and Knight perished in the wreckage. He received a posthumous mention in despatches. His crew thought it should have been the VC.

Curiously, Shannon's bomb-aimer, Sumpter, and Townsend's front gunner, Webb, were back with 617 Squadron in April 1945, and in the same crew that attacked

First and last: Len Sumpter (back row left) and Doug Webb (second right), who flew on the first 617 Squadron raid to the dams and the last of the Second World War against Hitler's Bavarian retreat near Berchtesgaden.

Far Left Wing Commander G. P. Gibson VC DSO & Bar DFC & Bar with his decorations after the Dams Raid.

Left A post-war photograph of Barnes Wallis, Chief of Aeronautical Research and Development for the British Aircraft Corporation (Weybridge) Ltd, 1945–71. Knighted in 1968, Wallis received a telegram from Bomber Harris that simply read: 'My Dear Sir'.

Hitler's Bavarian lair at Berchtesgaden. They therefore flew on the squadron's first and last operations of the Second World War.

Many of the aircrew who flew on Operation Chastise had distinguished post-war careers. Martin reached the rank of air marshal with a seat on the Air Force Board. His navigator, Leggo, entered politics in Australia, where the rear gunner, Simpson, became a successful barrister. Shannon was among several to enter the business world. Heal, Brown's navigator, returned to being a customs officer, and Hobday, Knight's navigator, to Lloyd's of London, where he managed the Aviation Department. Howard, Townsend's navigator, in recognition of his sterling work with the RAAF Association, would have a lake named after him at Bull Creek in Western Australia. McCarthy remained in the RCAF and, like Shannon's navigator, Walker, was promoted to wing commander. Oancia, Brown's bomb-aimer, qualified as a civil engineer. Ironically, one of his first jobs was to build a dam in northern Quebec.

Of the three main test pilots involved in perfecting 'Upkeep', Summers and Handasyde survived – Summers to fly the Viscount and Valiant prototypes. Longbottom was killed in January 1945 testing a Vickers Warwick. During the war Wallis designed a 6-ton version of his 1941 10-ton proposal. Codenamed 'Tallboy', it was used in November 1944 by 617 Squadron to sink the battleship *Tirpitz*, which so many had feared would be the target in May 1943. The squadron also destroyed the Bielefeld viaduct in western Germany in March 1945 with 'Grand Slam', the 10-ton bomb now at last available. Wallis's association with the squadron, to which he had effectively given birth, therefore continued throughout the war.

Wallis died in 1979, two years after 617 Squadron had been prominent in his ninetieth birthday celebrations. By then he had been knighted. In 1951 he was awarded £10,000 for his work on wartime bombs, and he used it to create a special foundation at his old school, Christ's Hospital, for the children of RAF personnel. Its badge has the breached Möhne Dam and '617' as the centrepiece.

617 Crews Engaged in Operation Chastise 16–17 May 1943

Aircraft (Wave)	Times: Take-off, Landing/ Approx crash	Pilot	Flight Engineer	Navigator
AJ-G (1) ED932/G	2139 0415	Wg Cdr G. P. Gibson DSO & Bar, DFC & Bar	Sgt J. Pulford	Plt Off H. T. Taerum RCAF
AJ-M (1) ED925/G	2139 0034	Flt Lt J. V. Hopgood DFC & Bar	Sgt C. Brennan	Fg Off K. Earnshaw RCAF
AJ-P (1) ED909/G	2139 0319	Flt Lt H. B. Martin DFC	Plt Off I. Whittaker	Flt Lt J. F. Leggo DFC, RAAF
AJ-A (1)* ED877/G	2147 0258	Sqn Ldr H. M. Young DFC & Bar	Sgt D. T. Horsfall	F/Sgt C. W. Roberts
AJ-J (1) ED906/G	2147 0311	Flt Lt D. J. H. Maltby DFC	Sgt W. Hatton	Sgt V. Nicholson
AJ-L (1) ED929/G	2147 0406	Flt Lt D. J. Shannon DFC, RAAF	Sgt R. J. Henderson	Fg Off D. R. Walker DFC, RCAF
AJ-Z (1)* ED937/G	2159 0236	Sqn Ldr H. E. Maudslay DFC	Sgt J. Marriott DFM	Fg Off R. A. Urquhart DFC, RCAF
AJ-B (1)* ED864/G	2159 0015	Flt Lt W. Astell DFC	Sgt J. Kinnear	Plt Off F. A. Wile RCAF
AJ-N (1) ED912/G	2159 0420	Plt Off L. G. Knight RAAF	Sgt R. E. Grayston	Fg Off H. S. Hobday
AJ-E (2)* ED927/G	2128 2350	Flt Lt R. N. G. Barlow DFC, RAAF	Plt Off S. L. Whillis	Fg Off P. S. Burgess
AJ-W (2) ED921/G	2129 0036	Flt Lt J. L. Munro RNZAF	Sgt F. E. Appleby	Fg Off F. G. Rumbles
AJ-K (2)* ED934/G	2130 2257	Plt Off V. W. Byers RCAF	Sgt A. J. Taylor	Fg Off J. H. Warner
AJ-H (2) ED936/G	2131 0047	Plt Off G. Rice	Sgt E. C. Smith	Fg Off R. MacFarlane
AJ-T (2) ED825/G	2201 0323	Flt Lt J. C. McCarthy DFC, RCAF	Sgt W. G. Radcliffe RCAF	F/Sgt D. A. MacLean RCAF
AJ-C (3) ED910/G	0009 0235	Plt Off W. H. T. Ottley DFC	Sgt R. Marsden	Fg Off J. K. Barrett DFC
AJ-S (3)* E D865/G	0011 0200	Plt Off L. J. Burpee DFM, RCAF	Sgt G. Pegler	Sgt T. Jaye
AJ-F (3) ED918/G	0012 0533	F/Sgt K. W. Brown RCAF	Sgt H. B. Feneron	Sgt D. P. Heal
AJ-O (3) E D886/G	0014 0615	F/Sgt W. C. Townsend DFM	Sgt D. J. D. Powell	Plt Off C. L. Howard RAAF
AJ-Y (3) ED924/G	0015 0530	F/Sgt C. T. Anderson	Sgt R. C. Paterson	Sgt J. P. Nugent

* The positions of the two gunners in these aircraft cannot be confirmed.

Wireless Operator	Bomb-aimer	Front gunner	Rear gunner
Flt Lt R. E. G. Hutchison DFC	Plt Off F. M. Spafford DFM, RAAF	F/Sgt G. A. Deering RCAF	Flt Lt R. D. Trevor Roper DFM
Sgt J. W. Minchin	F/ Sgt J. W. Fraser RCAF	Plt Off G. H. F. G. Gregory DFM	Plt Off A. F. Burcher DFM, RAAF
Fg Off L. Chambers RNZAF	Flt Lt R. C. Hay DFC, RAAF	Plt Off B. T. Foxlee DFM, RAAF	F/Sgt T. D. Simpson RAAF
Sgt L. W. Nichols	Fg Off V. S. MacCausland RCAF	Sgt G. A. Yeo	Sgt W. Ibbotson
Sgt A. J. B. Stone	Plt Off J. Fort	Sgt V. Hill	Sgt H. T. Simmonds
Fg Off B. Goodale DFC	F/Sgt L. J. Sumpter	Sgt B. Jagger	Fg Off J. Buckley
WO A. P. Cottam	Plt Off M. J. D. Fuller	Fg Off W. J. Tytherleigh DFC	Sgt N. R. Burrows
WO A. A. Garshowitz RCAF	Fg Off D. Hopkinson	F/Sgt F. A. Garbas RCAF	Sgt R. Bolitho
F/Sgt R. G. T. Kellow RAAF	Fg Off E. C. Johnson	Sgt F. E. Sutherland RCAF	Sgt H. E. O'Brien RCAF
Fg Off C. R. Williams DFC, RAAF	Plt Off A. Gillespie DFM	Fg Off H. S. Glinz RCAF	Sgt J. R. G. Liddell
WO P. E. Pigeon RCAF	Sgt J. H. Clay	Sgt W. Howarth	F/Sgt H. A. Weeks RCAF
Sgt J. Wilkinson	Plt Off A. N. Whittaker	Sgt C. McA. Jarvie	Flt Sgt J. McDowell RCAF
WO C. B. Gowrie RCAF	WO J. W. Thrasher RCAF	Sgt T. W. Maynard	Sgt S. Burns
F/Sgt L. Eaton	Sgt G. L. Johnson	Sgt R. Batson	Fg Off D. Rodger RCAF
Sgt J. Guterman DFM	F/Sgt T. B. Johnston	Sgt H. J. Strange	Sgt F. Tees
Plt Off L. G. Weller	F/Sgt J. L. Arthur RCAF	Sgt W. C. A. Long	WO J. G. Brady RCAF
Sgt H. J. Hewstone	Sgt S. Oancia RCAF	Sgt D. Allatson	F/Sgt G. S. MacDonald RCAF
F/Sgt G. A. Chalmers	Sgt C. E. Franklin DFM	Sgt D. E. Webb	Sgt R. Wilkinson
Sgt W. D. Bickle	Sgt G. J. Green	Sgt E. Ewan	Sgt A. W. Buck

All aircrew shown are RAF or RAF Volunteer Reserve unless indicated otherwise.

Index

Picture Credits

Archiv Ruhrtalsperrenverein 20 (top), 86; author's collection 20 (bottom), 24, 25, 29, 38 (bottom), 65, 155, 156, 160, 165, 186, 187 (right); Alex Bateman 42, 163; Patrick Bill 100, 101; BRE/Building Research Station 27 (top); Crown Copyright 46, 164 (top), 164 (bottom), 166, 172, 182-3; Andrew Hasson 146; Hulton Getty 16, 17 (top), 17 (bottom); Imperial War Museum 22, 28, 33, 36, 37 (top), 37 (bottom), 38 (top), 39, 56-7, 60-61, 70, 71, 74, 78-9, 85, 88, 90, 92, 93, 97, 126, 161, 162, 171, 173, 174, 175 (top), 175 (bottom), 176, 177, 185, 187 (left); Les Munro 40, 41; Public Record Office 179; Road Research Laboratory 27 (bottom); Dave Rodger 66; Tigress Productions 47, 49, 50, 51, 77, 78, 80 (top left, top right, centre left, centre right), 82, 102-3, 106, 148-9, 150-1, 152; Vickers (Aviation) Ltd 30, 31, 34, 53, 55, 170; Stuart Woods 44, 76, 80 (bottom); Ken Woroner 104, 105. The maps reproduced in Chapters 8, 9 and 10 are courtesy of the British Map Library.